FoxTrot Beyond a Doubt

Other FoxTrot Books by Bill Amend

FoxTrot
Pass the Loot
Black Bart Says Draw
Eight Yards, Down and Out
Bury My Heart at Fun-Fun Mountain
Say Hello to Cactus Flats
May the Force Be With Us, Please
Take Us to Your Mall
The Return of the Lone Iguana
At Least This Place Sells T-Shirts
Come Closer, Roger, There's a Mosquito on Your Nose
Welcome to Jasorassic Park

Anthologies

FoxTrot: The Works
FoxTrot *en masse*
Enormously FoxTrot
Wildly FoxTrot

FoxTrot Beyond a Doubt

by Bill Amend

Andrews and McMeel
A Universal Press Syndicate Company
Kansas City

FoxTrot is distributed internationally by Universal Press Syndicate.

ISBN: 0-8362-2694-1

Library of Congress Catalog Card Number: 96-79239

Printed on recycled paper.

99 00 01 BAM 10 9 8 7 6 5 4 3

Introduction

Look, I'll admit it. Being a cartoonist is a pretty great job.

Even if you took away all the supermodels, the World Series appearances, the Nobel Prizes, the gigs with Bruce, the space shuttle missions, the White House galas, and all the rest of the stuff you read about in the papers, I'd probably still want to do this for a living.

Sure, there are downsides. Like the realization that it took me something close to a bajillion hours to write and draw all the strips in a book that the average reader will finish in approximately 2.6 trips to the bathroom.

Or the weekly do-or-die deadlines that have caused me to break surely every traffic law on the books as I've raced "Bullitt"-like to my local FedEx station. (If my characters have ever appeared to you a little queasy, well, now you know why.)

Or that seemingly half the people I meet say they never read the comics and the rest, who do, invariably say something like, "FoxTrot. Hmm. Never heard of it." Ouch.

But I prefer to dwell on the positive aspects of my work. Like the fact that I can spend entire days playing video games and tell my wife with a straight face that I'm doing important research into the mind-set of my teenage characters.

Or that I can devise secret codes and distribute things like classified secrets to millions of readers worldwide right under their governments' noses. (Want to know the truth about Roswell? The CFR? Black helicopters? Stay tuned.)

Or the knowledge that the same sorts of super-brilliant math and physics professors who I could never seem to impress while a student, now frequently post clippings of my strip outside their office doors.

But the biggest, *biggest* plus of this job is one that I hope you can guess simply by reading FoxTrot: I have a whole lot of fun creating this strip. The same things that make a cartoon enjoyable to read typically make it enjoyable to write and draw and I'm praying that the reverse is also true. In other words, I hope you'll have equal fun reading this book. Even if only for 2.6 trips to the bathroom.

Guess I should wrap this up. I've got a pretty great job to get back to. Thanks for making it possible.

Bill Amend

TO MY
MANY TEACHERS
WITH THANKS
(AND APOLOGIES)

HOWDY, MA'AM.
JASON, WHAT ARE YOU DOING?!

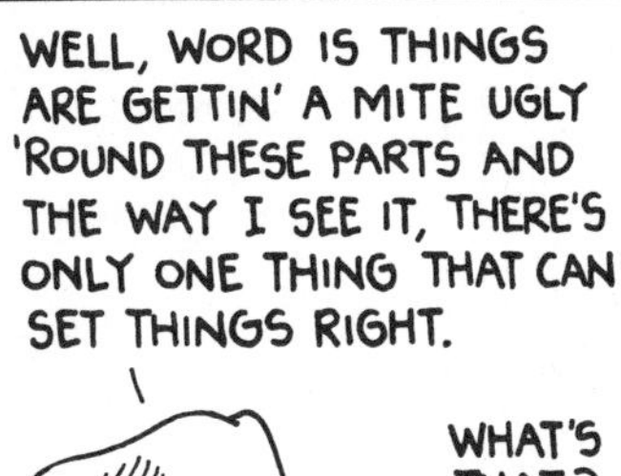
WELL, WORD IS THINGS ARE GETTIN' A MITE UGLY 'ROUND THESE PARTS AND THE WAY I SEE IT, THERE'S ONLY ONE THING THAT CAN SET THINGS RIGHT.

WHAT'S THAT?

(TA DA)
THE RETURN OF THE LONE IGUANA!
DIDN'T WE GO THROUGH THIS LAST SUMMER?

OK, THE RETURN OF THE RETURN OF THE LONE IGUANA.
YOU KNOW, IN CASE YOU THINK I ENJOY PEELING YOUR SISTER OFF THE CEILING...
AMEND

WHAT'S GOING ON?!

WHY IS THE WILLIAM TELL OVERTURE PLAYING ON THE STEREO AT SEVEN O'CLOCK IN THE MORNING?!
AMEND

THIS CAN'T BE HAPPENING! IT'S LIKE A BAD DREAM!

THE LONE IGUANA SAYS DON'T TOUCH THAT DIAL.
...ONLY WEIRDER.

PARDON ME, MISSY, BUT HAVE YOU SEEN THIS VARMINT?

SHE'S WANTED FOR ILLEGALLY IMPERSONATING A HORSE.

'COURSE SHE GOT THE FACE AND BUTT ALL MIXED UP.

...THAT AND ATTEMPTED MURDER.
JASON, GO AWAY.
AMEND

THIRTY MORE MINUTES...

TEN MORE MINUTES...

TWO MORE... ONE MORE... YEEHA! QUITTIN' TIME!

THIRTEEN MORE HOURS...
I HAD MORE, BUT PAIGE MADE ME EAT THEM.
AMEND

JASON, GO AWAY!

JASON, GO AWAY!
Toridos

JASON, GO AWAY!
AMEND

I CAN SEE WHERE THE "LONE" LABEL COMES FROM.

WHAT HAPPENED TO THE LONE IGUANA?
HE RODE OFF INTO THE SUNSET.

FINALLY.
ALL HE LEFT BEHIND WAS THIS SILVER SUCTION DART.

JASON, I CAN'T BELIEVE YOU'D GO TO ALL THE TROUBLE OF PAINTING ONE OF THESE.

THEN AGAIN...
I GUESS HE KNEW WERE-IGUANAS WERE AFOOT.
AMEND

FoxTrot

BILL AMEND

HEE HEE HEE...
WHAT'S SO FUNNY?

PAIGE LEFT HER OATMEAL UNATTENDED, SO I SPAT IN IT. NOW THE BOWL'S EMPTY, SO SHE MUST'VE EATEN IT. HEE HEE HEE.
PAIGE HAD EGGS FOR BREAKFAST.

EGGS?

I, ON THE OTHER HAND...
DID I SAY OATMEAL?... I MEANT WAFFLES...
AMEND

THIS MOVIE THEATER IS FREEZING!
NO KIDDING!

WHAT DO THEY DO – SET THE THERMOSTAT TO "ARCTIC ICE STORM"?!
BRRR!

I MEAN, MY TEETH ARE CHATTERING!
MINE ARE TOO. LET'S JUST GO.

I SWEAR, YOU NEED A COAT IN THERE!
OR SOME-THING...
AMEND

YOU KNOW, IT'S REALLY CONVENIENT THAT YOUR MOM IS A NURSE.
NOW REMEMBER, THIS PARKING LOT HAS SPEED BUMPS...
The Flaming Blur
AMEND

From the desk of
Jason Fox
From the desk of
Jason Fox
From the desk of
Jason Fox
From the desk of
Jason Fox
From the desk of
Jason Fox

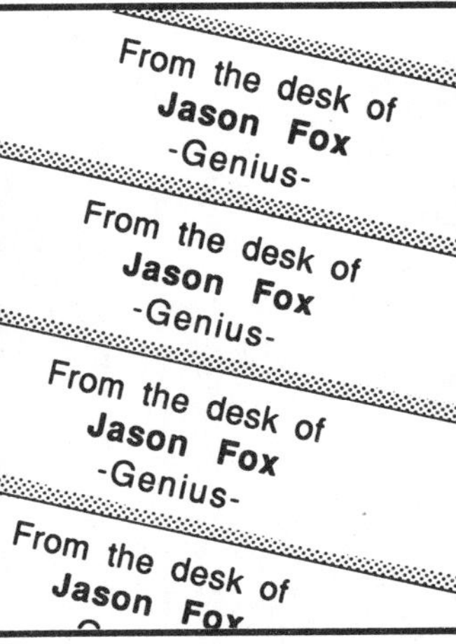

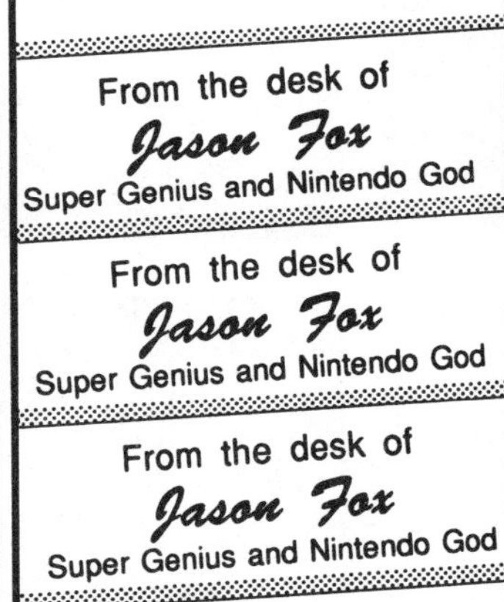

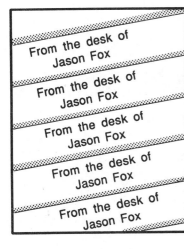

FoxTrot
BILL AMEND

OH, MAN, I HAD THE WORST DREAM LAST NIGHT.

SCHOOL STARTED TWO WEEKS EARLY AND THEY CHANGED MY SCHEDULE SO I HAD NOTHING BUT MATH CLASSES.

WITH QUIZZES EVERY DAY.

ICK. I'M SO GLAD I WOKE UP.
NO DOUBT.
OH, MAN, I HAD THE BEST DREAM LAST NIGHT.
AMEND

JASON FOX, YOU'VE SPENT PRACTICALLY YOUR WHOLE SUMMER COOPED UP IN FRONT OF THAT COMPUTER!

ENOUGH ALREADY! I WANT YOU BOYS TO PLAY OUTSIDE AND GET SOME FRESH AIR IN THOSE LUNGS FOR A CHANGE! LET'S GO!

AND DON'T COME BACK UNTIL DINNERTIME!

THREE WORDS: HALLELUJAH FOR LAPTOPS.
I'VE GOT YOUR SPARE BATTERY CHARGING UP IN THE GARAGE.
AMEND

WHERE'S PAIGE?
SHE WENT OUT TO BUY BINDER PAPER.

WHAT? I TOLD HER WE'D DO ALL HER BACK-TO-SCHOOL SHOPPING **NEXT** WEEK!

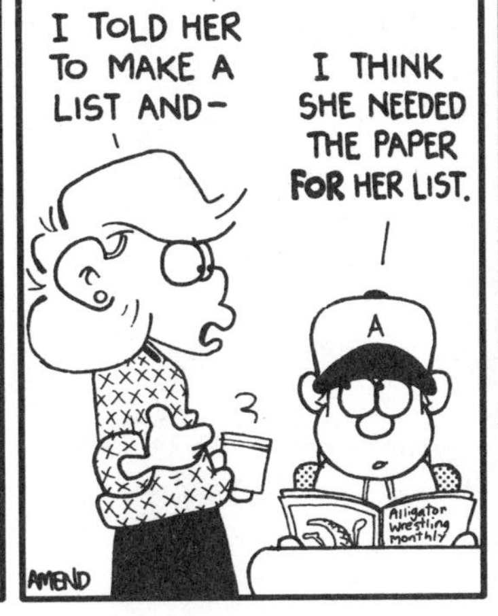
I TOLD HER TO MAKE A LIST AND—
I THINK SHE NEEDED THE PAPER **FOR** HER LIST.
AMEND

BUT I'VE GOT PLENTY OF PAPER...
DEFINE "PLENTY."
WHY IS PAIGE DRAG-GING A BIG BOX UP THE DRIVEWAY?

QUINCY, SHAKE.

LIE DOWN. ROLL OVER. HEEL. PLAY DEAD. JUMP.
Deep Space

YOU ARE SO PATHETIC.
Velociraptor

I SUPPOSE "ATTACK" IS OUT OF THE QUESTION.
AMEND

WHAT MOVIE DID YOU GET?
"RETURN TO THE PLANET OF THE MAGGOTS."

EEW! GROSS! SICK!

I CAN'T BELIEVE YOU WOULD RENT THIS! I CAN'T BELIEVE YOU WOULD ACTUALLY PAY MONEY TO PUT SOMETHING THIS DISGUSTING ON OUR TV! I CAN'T BELIEVE A MOVIE LIKE THIS EVEN EXISTS!

AMEND

SO, DID IT JUST START?
I'LL REWIND IT. THE OPENING'S PRETTY IMPORTANT.

HOW DO FOOTBALL PLAYERS REMEMBER ALL THESE PLAYS?
HOW DO FOOTBALL PLAYERS REMEMBER THEIR NAMES?
AMEND

FoxTrot
BILL AMEND

I CAN'T WAIT FOR SCHOOL TO START...

I REALLY CAN'T WAIT FOR SCHOOL TO START...

I REALLY, REALLY, **REEEALLY** CAN'T WAIT FOR SCHOOL TO START...
PETER, THIS IS SO UNLIKE YOU!

READY FOR BACK-TO-SCHOOL SHOPPING, ROUND XII?
PAIGE, CAN'T WE TAKE **ONE** DAY OFF??
AH...
AMEND

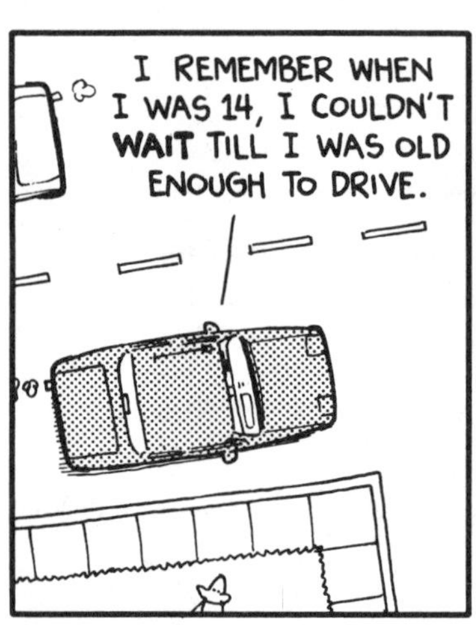
I REMEMBER WHEN I WAS 14, I COULDN'T **WAIT** TILL I WAS OLD ENOUGH TO DRIVE.

WHEN I WAS 15, I WAS PRACTICALLY GOING OUT OF MY **MIND** WITH ANTICIPATION.

AND NOW THAT I FINALLY **AM** 16...
AMEND

PETER, QUIT YAPPING AND STEP ON IT. THE MALL OPENS IN TWO MINUTES.
...I CAN'T WAIT TILL **YOU** ARE OLD ENOUGH TO DRIVE.

WELL, PETER, YOU'RE ONE LUCKY BROTHER.
OH?

MY SHOPPING LIST IS TWICE AS LONG AS USUAL, MOM IS LETTING ME USE ONE OF HER CREDIT CARDS AND I PACKED US A COUPLE OF ENERGY BARS SO WE CAN SHOP RIGHT THROUGH LUNCHTIME.

AMEND

IN OTHER WORDS, YOU'RE GOING TO BE IN THIS MALL **ALL DAY LONG**!!!

OH, WAIT—WE HAVE DIFFERING VIEWS ON "LUCK"...
SOMEONE JUST SHOOT ME, PLEASE.

LET'S SEE... IF I GET THIS BLACK BELT, I CAN'T WEAR THE TAN SHOES AND THE BROWN PURSE GOES OUT THE WINDOW.

BUT... IF I DON'T GET THE TAN SHOES, I COULD GET THOSE CUTE RED PANTS THAT WOULD LOOK GREAT WITH THIS BELT AND WHICH HAD THAT HOT MATCHING SWEATER-VEST...

IF I DO GO WITH THE RED PANTS, HOWEVER, I'D HAVE TO START ALL OVER IN THE EARRING DEPARTMENT BECAUSE THOSE BLUE ONES WOULDN'T MATCH. HMM...

IT'S A LOT LIKE CHESS.
SO WHY DOES IT FEEL LIKE HANGMAN?
AMEND

WHEW. I'M BEAT.
MALL DIRECTORY
1ST LEVEL

I SWEAR, WE MUST'VE WALKED UP AND DOWN THIS MALL 20 TIMES TODAY AT LEAST. THINK HOW MANY MILES THAT IS!

MY FEET ARE KILLING ME... MY BACK IS KILLING ME... MY LEGS ARE JUST PLAIN POOPED...
MALL DIRECTORY
1ST LEVEL

THANK HEAVENS WE'RE DOWN TO THE LAST PAGE OF MY SHOPPING LIST.
WILL THERE BE ANY STORES THAT SELL ASPIRIN?
AMEND

I CAN'T BELIEVE I'VE ACTUALLY FINISHED ALL OF MY BACK-TO-SCHOOL SHOPPING!

I'VE GOT THE PERFECT BACK-TO-SCHOOL OUTFIT... THE PERFECT BACK-TO-SCHOOL PURSE... AN ADORABLE BACK-TO-SCHOOL HAIR-CARE ENSEMBLE... EVERYTHING!

I, PAIGE FOX, AM NOW READY FOR SCHOOL TO START!
WHAT ABOUT GETTING NOTEBOOKS AND STUFF?

OOPS.
IF YOU THINK FOR ONE SECOND THAT WE'RE DRIVING BACK TO THAT MALL...
AMEND

FoxTrot
BILL AMEND

This is your brain →

This is your brain on drugs →

This is my sister's brain →

YOU ALREADY FORGOT YOUR LOCKER COM-BINATION?!
MY MEMORY IS REALLY BAD, OK?

PAIGE, WHY DIDN'T YOU WRITE IT ON YOUR HAND OR SOMETHING, THEN?
I WISH I **HAD**.
AMEND

OH, WAIT– I DID.

YOU WEREN'T KIDDING ABOUT YOUR MEMORY.
SHOOT–NOW WHICH ONE WAS MY LOCKER?...

SO, DO WE WANT TO SIT IN THE FRONT OF THE CLASS WHERE WE'LL BE PERCEIVED AS NERDS, IN THE BACK WHERE WE'LL BE PERCEIVED AS SLACK-ERS OR SOMEWHERE IN THE MIDDLE WHERE WE WON'T BE PERCEIVED AS MUCH OF ANYTHING?

C'MON, ASHLEY, LET'S SIT UP FRONT.
AMEND

CALL ME NERD BOY.
HOW DID WE MAKE DECISIONS BEFORE HORMONES?

HI. I WAS WONDERING IF IT WAS POSSIBLE TO CHANGE SOME OF MY CLASSES.
WHAT SORT OF CHANGES DO YOU HAVE IN MIND?
REGISTRAR

WELL, YOU'VE GOT ME IN REGULAR ENGLISH AND I'D LIKE TO BE IN THE COLLEGE PREP CLASS... I'M IN ALGEBRA AND I WANT TO MOVE UP TO GEOMETRY... AND I HOPE YOU CAN SOMEHOW GET ME INTO THE 2ND-YEAR FRENCH CLASS.
I'LL SEE WHAT I CAN DO.
I TAKE IT YOU'VE LOOKED INTO THESE CLASSES.
REGISTRAR

ENOUGH TO SEE ALL THE CUTE BOYS.
AND ISN'T THAT WHAT SCHOOL IS ALL ABOUT?...
REGISTRAR
AMEND

I JUST LOVE GETTING A BRAND-NEW TEXTBOOK.

I LOVE MAKING A BOOK-COVER FOR IT OUT OF AN OLD GROCERY BAG... I LOVE THE CRACKING SOUND IT MAKES THE FIRST TIME YOU OPEN IT... I LOVE ALL OF THE CLEAN, CRISP PAGES AND THE WAY IT SMELLS...

GEOMETRY

I LOVE IT!
I LOVE IT!
I LOVE IT!

LET'S JUST SAY IT WAS A ONE-NIGHT STAND.
I SEE I'LL BE WRITING A CHECK TO THE MATH DEPARTMENT AGAIN.

IT'S FUNNY HOW SUMMER KINDA CLOUDS YOUR MEMORIES.

YOU FORGET HOW ANNOYING MOST OF YOUR FRIENDS ARE... YOU FORGET HOW HARD IT IS TO WAKE UP FOR SCHOOL... YOU FORGET WHAT A PAIN DOING HOMEWORK REALLY IS...

HUKGACHK!

...YOU FORGET THE IMPORTANCE OF BRINGING A BAG LUNCH...
WHAT IS THIS STUFF?!

WHAT A WEEK THIS WAS.

I HAD TO READ AN ENTIRE SHAKESPEARE PLAY, WRITE A TWO-PAGE ESSAY ON CRIME, MEMORIZE EVERY ATOMIC SYMBOL AND STAND UP IN CLASS AND DEBATE SOCIAL DARWINISM.

AND I'M NOT EVEN GOING TO DISCUSS WHAT I HAD TO DO FOR **MATH**.

WE LEARNED TO PLAY THE AUTOHARP.

WHAT A WEEKEND THIS WILL BE.
THEN WE PLAYED DODGE-BALL...

FoxTrot

BILL AMEND

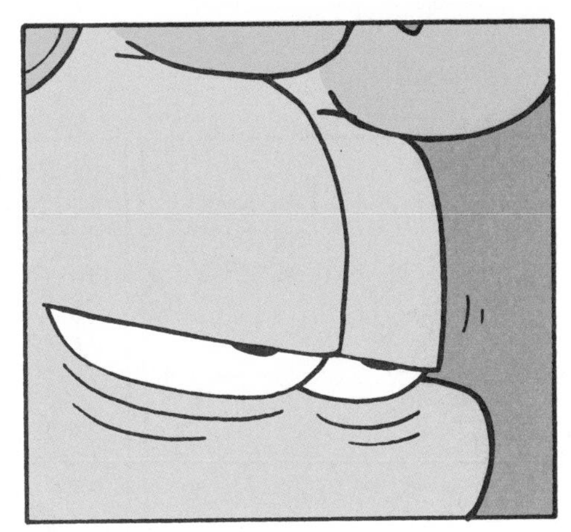

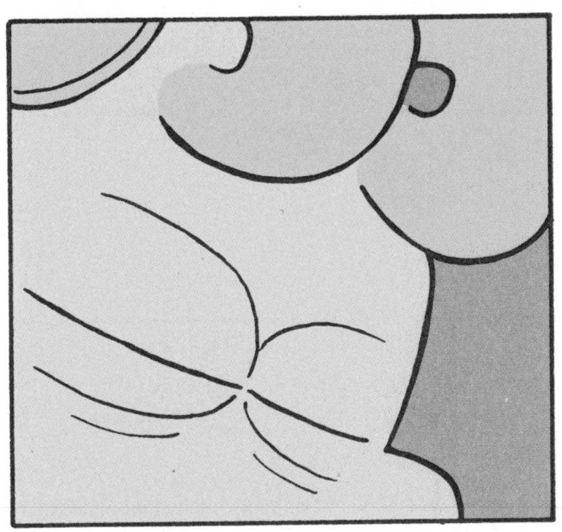

Blink Blink Blink

SNQRZZZzz

Blink Blink Blink

SNQRZZZzz

WHUMP!

DROOOOOOOOL...

I'VE GOT TO STOP CHEWING GUM WHEN I READ.
I FOUND A CROWBAR.
WORLD HISTORY
AMEND

WHERE'S JASON?
UPSTAIRS ON THE COMPUTER.

HE TALKED ME INTO SUBSCRIBING TO COMPUNET. IT'S THAT NEW ONLINE INFORMATION SERVICE. HE'S BEEN USING IT ALL AFTERNOON.

IT'S REALLY QUITE REMARKABLE. JASON WAS TELLING ME HOW HE CAN USE IT TO ACCESS THE INTERNET, WHICH WILL CONNECT HIM TO UNIVERSITIES, GOVERNMENT AGENCIES AND PRIVATE COMPUTERS ALL OVER THE WORLD. JUST THINK OF ALL THE FASCINATING THINGS OUR KIDS CAN NOW LEARN!

MISS OCTOBER SURE HAS BIG HOOTERS.
I WONDER IF THAT AFFECTS DOWNLOAD TIME...
AMEND

SO THIS IS THE FAMOUS INTERNET.

THE DATA SUPERHIGHWAY... THE INFORMATION AUTOBAHN... THE BULLET TRAIN TO CYBERVILLE...

COOL.

ACTUALLY, DAD, THE COMPUTER'S NOT TURNED ON.
I THOUGHT MAYBE YOU WERE IN A TUNNEL.
AMEND

WELCOME TO COMPUNET.

YOU HAVE 65,031 WAITING MESSAGES.

MAYBE SETTING MY USERNAME TO "FABIO" WASN'T SUCH A HOT IDEA.
DIANE@NASA.GOV WISHES TO CHAT.
LUCILLE@OSU.EDU WISHES TO CHAT.
JOYCE@UPS.COM WISHES TO CHAT.
AMEND

THIS COMPUNET IS REALLY COOL.
NERD.

YOU CAN ACCESS THE INTERNET...
NERD.
YOU CAN CHAT WITH FAMOUS CARTOONISTS...
NERD.
YOU CAN READ BACK-ISSUE ARTICLES FROM MODEL ROCKETRY MAGAZINE...
NERD.

THEY'VE EVEN GOT AN ONLINE MALL WHERE YOU CAN GO SHOPPING.
AMEND

NERDETTE.
GO FIND OUT WHAT MOM'S CREDIT LIMIT IS.

JASON, WILL YOU PLEASE TURN OFF THE MODEM? I NEED TO USE THE TELEPHONE.
BUT I'M RIGHT IN THE MIDDLE OF A DOWNLOAD!

COMPUNET JUST STARTED CARRYING BLACK BANSHEE COMIC BOOK PREVIEWS. I'M DOWNLOADING THE FIRST THREE PAGES OF NEXT MONTH'S ISSUE.
AMEND

HOW LONG WILL THAT TAKE?
WELL, LET'S SEE... I STARTED AT ABOUT 4:15...

HOW'S MIDNIGHT SOUND?
JASON, ARE YOU FAMILIAR WITH A LITTLE THING CALLED A PHONE JACK?

JASON, I JUST GOT OUR FIRST COMPUNET BILL.

I THOUGHT I MADE IT CLEAR THAT THE FLAT $8.95 MONTHLY FEE ONLY COVERS THE FIRST SIX HOURS OF USE!
SIX HOURS EACH MONTH?! I THOUGHT IT WAS SIX HOURS EACH DAY!
AMEND

UH-OH...

NOW, THEN, YOUR ALLOWANCE IS ALREADY BEING WITHHELD THROUGH YOUR SOPHOMORE YEAR IN COLLEGE.
IS THIS A BAD TIME TO SUGGEST YOU BUY A FASTER MODEM?

FoxTrot
BILL AMEND

OK, NOW IN THIS SCENE, THE T. REX CHASES THE WOUNDED BRACHIOSAURUS OVER THE HILL.
105 EXT. JUNGLE

LET ME EXPLAIN YOUR MOTIVATIONS...

WATCH OUT FOR THE LIGHTS– THEY'RE HOT.
WHAT ARE YOU DOING?

I'M MAKING A STOP-MOTION ANIMATED DINOSAUR MOVIE.

I'M CALLING IT "MESOZOIC PARK," WHICH IS ACTUALLY WHAT "JURASSIC PARK" SHOULD HAVE BEEN CALLED.
DON'T TOUCH THEM – THEY'RE CLAY.

YOU SEE, OUT OF THE SIX SPECIES OF DINOSAURS FEATURED IN THAT MOVIE, ONLY TWO– BRACHIOSAURUS AND DILOPHOSAURUS – CAN BE TRACED TO THE JURASSIC PERIOD.

THE OTHERS – TRICERATOPS, T.REX, VELOCIRAPTOR AND GALLIMIMUS – WERE ALL FROM THE LATE CRETACEOUS PERIOD, SOME 75 MILLION YEARS LATER.
THE MESOZOIC PERIOD INCLUDES BOTH.
Mesozoic
Triassic
Jurassic
Cretaceous

SO, WHILE STEVEN SPIELBERG'S MOVIE MAY BE MORE REALISTIC THAN MINE, MINE IS AT LEAST MORE ACCURATE.
DID THE MESOZOIC PERIOD HAVE TAR PITS?

AAAA! MY T. REX HERD IS MELTING!
SAY, ISN'T THIS MOM'S GOOD TABLECLOTH?
AMEND

MOM, I DON'T FEEL SO GOOD.

MY STOMACH'S KINDA QUEASY, MY FOREHEAD'S ALL CLAMMY AND MY HEART IS GOING A MILLION BEATS PER SECOND.

I THINK I MAY EVEN THROW UP.
AMEND

YOU ATE JASON'S CEREAL AGAIN, DIDN'T YOU?
WE WERE OUT OF WHEATIES.
HOW DO YOU SUPPOSE THEY GET GRAIN TO GLOW IN THE DARK?

JASON, HE'S SICK.
PETER GETS TO STAY HOME FROM SCHOOL?!

THAT WONDERFUL GLOW-IN-THE-DARK CEREAL OF YOURS MADE HIM THROW UP.

WHAT?! I EAT TWO BOWLS OF THAT STUFF EVERY DAY AND I HAVEN'T BEEN SICK TO MY STOMACH **ONCE**!
AMEND

MAYBE I SHOULD BE EATING THREE...
I THINK IT'S TIME I STOPPED TAKING YOU SHOPPING.

I CAN'T BELIEVE ONE BOWL OF CEREAL MADE ME THIS SICK.
Pepto Plus

WHAT'S IN THIS STUFF, ANYHOW?

Radioactive Sugar Nuggets

I GUESS I SHOULD BE HAPPY IT MADE ME **ONLY** THIS SICK.
NOW AREN'T YOU GLAD YOU TOOK THE **ADVANCED** CHEMISTRY CLASS?
AMEND

AAAA! MY STOMACH!

AAAA! MY HEAD!

AAAA! MY STOMACH **AND** HEAD!

PEOPLE WHO ARE SICK SHOULD **NOT** WATCH C-SPAN.
CLICK
BRRR... I'M GETTING CHILLS...
AMEND

NEXT ON "GERALDO": NYMPHOMANIAC LIBRARIANS AND THE BOOKS THAT TURN THEM ON.

(CLICK) NEXT ON "SALLY": THE DIRTY TRUTH BEHIND FEMALE MUD WRESTLING.
(CLICK) NEXT ON "MAURY": PERFORMANCE ART OR GIRLIE STRIP SHOW - YOU DECIDE.
(CLICK) NEXT ON "PHIL": UNIVERSITY WOMEN WHO POSE FOR PLAYBOY.

GOOD LORD - WHAT IS THIS WORLD COMING TO?!

IT'S GOTTEN TO WHERE A FELLOW NEEDS FIVE OR SIX VCRs!
BUT FIRST, THIS MESSAGE FROM MAIDENFORM.
AMEND

MOM, IT'S INCREDIBLE!

I MEAN, THAT I COULD FEEL SO **SICK** THIS MORNING AND YET FEEL SO **GREAT** RIGHT NOW! IT'S AMAZING!

LOOK AT ME DANCE - I **MUST** BE CURED! HALLELUJAH! O HAPPY DAY!
PETER, IF YOU WERE TOO SICK FOR SCHOOL, YOU'RE TOO SICK FOR THE MOVIES.

BUT MOMMM... "BLOODSPORT VII" OPENS TONIGHT!
YOU KNOW, FOR SOMEONE WHO CLAIMS TO HAVE BEEN QUEASY ALL DAY...
AMEND

FoxTrot
BILL AMEND

Ocelot

Giant Panda

Gray Wolf

Bengal Tiger

California Condor

Black Rhino

Humpback Whale

Peter Fox

I CAME UP WITH THIS GREAT NEW SYSTEM FOR DOING MY HOMEWORK.
OH?

RATHER THAN ALWAYS WAITING TO THE LAST MINUTE TO DO STUFF, I'M GONNA START ON MY ASSIGNMENTS AS SOON AS I GET HOME EVERY DAY. I FIGURE IT'S BOUND TO IMPROVE THE QUALITY OF MY WORK.

NO MORE DELAYS... NO MORE PROCRASTINATION... NO MORE EXCUSES. YEE HA!
AMEND

WHAT HAPPENED TO YOUR NEW SYSTEM?
I'M STARTING IT TOMORROW.
TORIDOS

JOHNSON, YOU'RE GOING TO HAVE TO REDO THIS REPORT.
WHAT DO YOU MEAN?

IT'S GOT SPELLING MISTAKES IN JUST ABOUT EVERY SENTENCE. IT'S TOTALLY UNACCEPTABLE.

"ACCOMADATE"?! "INDEPENDANT"?! "BOTTEM"?! IT'S LIKE A THIRD-GRADER WROTE IT!
HEY, DON'T BLAME ME...

THIS STUPID COMPUTER DIDN'T COME WITH A SPELLCHECKER.
LET ME SPELL SOMETHING OUT FOR YOU.
AMEND

JASON, WHERE ARE YOU GOING WITH THOSE TOOLS?

YOU TOLD ME TO MAKE MY BED.
AMEND

I WAS THINKING OF USING CHERRY WOOD WITH A NICE MAHOGANY FINISH. OR WOULD THAT BE TOO DARK?

I WANT THOSE TOOLS BACK IN THE GARAGE, NOW!
SO YOU'RE TELLING ME TO NOT MAKE MY BED?..

HI, DADDY! YOU'RE HOME EARLY!

YOU MUST'VE SENSED I WAS COOKING DINNER TONIGHT AND YOU WANTED TO RUSH RIGHT HOME AND BE FIRST IN LINE.

AMEND

THINK ABOUT IT! HOW ELSE CAN YOU EXPLAIN IT?!

I GOT YOUR MESSAGE. THIS WAS THE BIGGEST BOTTLE OF ASPIRIN THEY HAD.
IS SHE STILL FRYING THE SALAD?

SO MUCH FOR THE "LET'S CHUG A POT OF COFFEE BEFORE THE MATH TEST" STRATEGY.
IS THERE A WOODPECKER IN HERE?
TAP TAP TAP TAP TAP TAP TAP TAP TAP
AMEND

AMEND

WHAT A GLORIOUS DAY.
WHAT KIND OF DERANGED MIND WOULD PILE LEAVES ON TOP OF DOG DOO?

FoxTrot

BILL AMEND

NGRESS
PING

program Jason1 (output);
var i : integer;
begin
for i:= 1 to 100 do
writeln ('I will not shoot ¬
rubber bands in class.');
end.

NGRESS
Run

PRINTZZZZ
PRINTZZZZ
PRINTZZZZ
PRINTZZZZ
PRINTZZZZ

rk:
ad Chap. 2
CAN I GO HOME NOW?
JASON, I MEANT WRITE IT BY **HAND**.
AMEND

WHAT ARE YOU DOING?
I HEARD THAT THE GUY WHO DRAWS "THE FAR SIDE" IS RETIRING AT THE END OF THE YEAR.
A

GARY LARSON? YEAH, I HEARD THAT TOO. SO?
WELL, I FIGURE THAT JUST BECAUSE HE'S QUITTING, IT DOESN'T MEAN THAT "THE FAR SIDE" HAS TO END. I'LL JUST TAKE IT OVER FOR HIM. I'M PUTTING TOGETHER A SAMPLE BATCH NOW.

THINK ABOUT IT! OVERNIGHT, YOUR LITTLE BROTHER COULD BECOME ONE OF THE WORLD'S MOST WIDELY READ CARTOONISTS! I'D BE FAMOUS! PEOPLE WOULD BE BEATING A PATH TO OUR DOOR!
AMEND

WITH PITCHFORKS AND TORCHES, MOST LIKELY.
HEE HEE HEE— IF YOU THINK THAT ONE'S GROSS...
A

The Far Side II
by Jason Fox
AMEND

Dang, Zeke, but that is one ugly cow!
Jason

The Far Side II
by Jason Fox
AMEND

Wait a minute... this can't be Earth — Earth has humans.
map
Jason

The Far Side II
by Jason Fox
AMEND

There goes my appetite.
Jason

The Far Side II
by Jason Fox
AMEND

It's said, Jenkins, that entering this tomb brings a curse.
Hi! I'm your new sister!
Jason

SO HOW'S THE CARTOONING BIZ?
I THINK, IN RETROSPECT, IT WAS A MISTAKE TO FEATURE PAIGE SO PROMINENTLY IN MY SUBSTITUTE "FAR SIDES."
Roads and Tracks

WHY? TOO REPETITIVE?
NO...
TOO HARD TO DRAW?
NO...
TOO INSIDE-JOKEY?
NO...

LET ME REPHRASE THAT: ...MY FORMERLY UNSHREDDED SUBSTITUTE "FAR SIDES."
Roads and Tracks

THAT WOULD EXPLAIN THE PILE OF CONFETTI.
FORTUNATELY, I HAVE PHOTOCOPIES.
YOU MIGHT WANT TO REPHRASE THAT, TOO.
AMEND

FoxTrot
BILL AMEND

HAVE YOU SEEN MY PUMPKIN ANYWHERE?
NO.

HAVE YOU SEEN MY PUMPKIN ANYWHERE?
NO.

HOW COULD I HAVE LOST MY PUMPKIN?! I JUST CARVED IT!
AMEND

ASK ME IF **I'VE** SEEN IT.
YOU LIVE FOR THIS WEEK, DON'T YOU?

WHAT ARE YOU DOING?
RIGGING UP SOME ROBOT ZOMBIES FOR THE FRONT YARD.

WHEN THE TRICK-OR-TREATERS BREAK THE INFRA-RED BEAM OUT BY THE MAILBOX, THE TAPE DECK KICKS IN, THE EERIE MUSIC STARTS, AND ONE BY ONE THESE MOTORIZED ARMS POP OUT OF THE LAWN. THEN THE FUN REALLY BEGINS.

AMEND

I SURE HOPE I CAN THROW THESE COW GUTS WITH ACCURACY.
Lou's Fresh Meat

YOU KNOW, THE IDEA ISN'T TO PREVENT KIDS FROM EVEN MAKING IT TO OUR FRONT DOOR...
DID YOU SEE ALL THE HUMONGOUS CANDY BARS MOM BOUGHT?!

WHO SUCKED ALL THE FILLING OUT OF THE TWINKIES?!
HURRY, OR WE REALLY **WILL** NEED COFFINS.
Twinkies
Jason
AMEND

WHOA, PETER! GREAT COSTUME!

I MEAN, HOW DID YOU EVER THINK OF THAT?!— THE LITTLE STEVEN SPIELBERG AND MICHAEL CRICHTON DOLLS ARE A STROKE OF IRONIC GENIUS! IT'S BRILLIANT! IT'S THE BEST HALLOWEEN COSTUME EVER!

I BOW IN HUMBLE AWE, O AMAZING OLDER SIBLING.
I'M NOT PETER. I'M PAIGE.

WHAT'S WITH THE WHITE MAKE-UP? ARE YOU DRESSING UP AS A GHOST?
THIS ISN'T MAKE-UP.
AMEND

I CAN'T DECIDE WHETHER TO CALL IT "PUMPKINMATION" OR "JACK-O-MATION."
ABOUT THIS PRODUCE BILL...
AMEND

I JUST DON'T KNOW WHAT I'M GOING TO DO ABOUT HALLOWEEN CANDY THIS YEAR.

HERE IT IS, TWO DAYS BEFORE HALLOWEEN AND THERE ARE NO MORE CHOCOLATE BARS, PEANUT BUTTER CUPS, SWEET-TARTS OR GUMMI WORMS! ALL THAT'S LEFT ARE A FEW RANDOM PACKS OF GUM!

IN THE STORES?
AMEND

IN OUR CANDY BOWL!
AHH.
WE'RE OUT OF GUM.

FoxTrot
BILL AMEND

WHERE'D YOU GET THE VIDEO CAMERA?
IT'S THE SCHOOL'S.

I'M DOING A PROJECT FOR MY CONTEMPORARY CULTURE CLASS.

I'M MAKING A PARODY OF MTV'S "THE REAL WORLD." IT'S THIS PSEUDO-DOCUMENTARY ON MTV WHERE EVERYONE SEEMS TO LIVE REALLY HIP, EVENTFUL LIVES. I'M MAKING MY OWN VERSION TO SHOW JUST HOW BORING REAL LIFE REALLY IS.
AMEND

MOM, DO WE HAVE A GEIGER COUNTER ANYWHERE?
GOOD LUCK.
LET'S GO VISIT PAIGE...

BRAAAP!
AMEND

SO WHAT'S WITH THE VIDEO CAMERA?
I'M TAPING STUFF FOR SCHOOL.

THE BURP I'LL EDIT OUT, BUT THE BUG EYES I'M **KEEPING**!
GIMME THAT THING!

CRUNCH CRUNCH CRUNCH CRUNCH

CRUNCH CRUNCH CRUNCH CRUNCH

CRUNCH CRUNCH CRUNCH...
AMEND

THIS IS NOT GOING QUITE ACCORDING TO SCRIPT...
DOCUMENTARIES DON'T HAVE SCRIPTS.

PETER, WHY ARE YOU VIDEO-TAPING ME?
IT'S FOR SCHOOL.

FOR A CLASS?
YES.

SO YOU'RE GOING TO SHOW THIS TO A WHOLE GROUP OF YOUR PEERS?
YUP.
AMEND

...THEN IN SIXTH GRADE, PETER'S BED-WETTING GOT A LITTLE BETTER...
I KNOW THIS THING HAS A REWIND BUTTON SOMEWHERE...

SAY HELLO TO THE NEXT BRANDO.
WHY? DID PETER VIDEOTAPE YOU TOO?
Baseball Illustrated

ME TOO?! ANDY, HE SAID I WAS THE BEST SUBJECT YET! THE CRÈME DE LA CRÈME! THE SHOW-STOPPING STAR!
AMEND

HE SAID MY PERFORMANCE VIRTUALLY GUARANTEED HIM AN "A" ON THIS ASSIGNMENT.
ROGER, HE'S MAKING A DOCUMENTARY ABOUT HOW BORING THE REAL WORLD IS.

HEY, STARDOM IS STARDOM.
WHAT-EVER YOU SAY, MARLON.
DAD, CAN WE RESHOOT THAT BIT WHERE YOU TALK ABOUT ANNUITIES?
Baseball Illustrated

SO HOW'D YOUR CLASS LIKE YOUR VIDEO PROJECT?
WELL, ON ONE HAND, YOU'D HAVE TO SAY I SUCCEEDED ADMIRABLY.

I SET OUT TO DOCUMENT JUST HOW BORING THE REAL "REAL WORLD" IS, AND MY VIDEO DID THAT VERY WELL. VERY, VERY WELL. TOO WELL.

HOW SO?
LET'S JUST SAY THE SNORING DROWNED OUT THE DIALOGUE.

DON'T TAKE IT TOO HARD—KIDS ARE ALWAYS FALLING ASLEEP DURING SCHOOL MOVIES.
BUT MY TEACHER ISN'T A KID.
AMEND

FoxTrot

BILL AMEND

I DON'T KNOW WHAT I LIKE BEST ABOUT THIS SHOW.

ITS TWISTING STORY LINES... ITS DIABOLICAL CHARACTERS... ITS HUNKY MALE ACTORS...
AAAA! WHAT ARE YOU WATCHING?!? MONDAY NIGHT FOOTBALL IS ON!
AMEND

...ITS DRAMATIC POWER...
THAT'D BE MY VOTE.
SUPPOSE I WERE TO PAY YOU KIDS $5 APIECE...

MOM! MOM! LOOK WHAT I GOT FROM MARCUS!

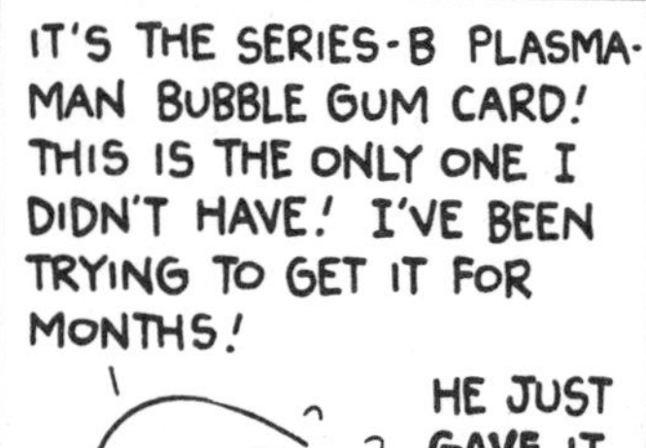
IT'S THE SERIES-B PLASMA-MAN BUBBLE GUM CARD! THIS IS THE ONLY ONE I DIDN'T HAVE! I'VE BEEN TRYING TO GET IT FOR MONTHS!

HE JUST GAVE IT TO YOU?

WELL, NO, I HAD TO TRADE HIM SOMETHING FOR IT.
ANOTHER CARD?
AMEND

HONESTLY.
IT'S NOT LIKE PAIGE RIDES IT MUCH.

MY STUPID ENGLISH TEACHER HAS LOST HIS MIND!
NOW WHAT?

HE EXPECTS US TO READ THIS FAT 400-PAGE BOOK PRACTICALLY OVERNIGHT!
OUCH. WHEN'S IT DUE? FRIDAY?

UM, NO...
MONDAY?
AMEND

LOOK, NEVER MIND.
TUESDAY?
I HEAR YOU HAVE TO READ SOME BOOK BY NEW YEAR'S.

COFFEEEEE...
THE POT'S OVER BY THE FRIDGE.

COFFEEEEE...
THE FRIDGE IS OVER THERE.

COFFEEEEE...
SEE THAT THING WITH THE LITTLE RED LIGHT?

"MORNING OF THE LIVING DEAD."
ROGER, THAT'S THE ANSWERING MACHINE.
GLUG GLUG GLUG
AMEND

TODAY IN THE O.J. SIMPSON TRIAL...
CLICK

TODAY IN THE O.J. SIMPSON TRIAL...
CLICK

CLICK
CLICK
CLICK
CLICK
CLICK
CLICK
TRIAL...
TODAY IN THE O.J. SIMPSON TRIAL...
TODAY IN THE O.J. SIMPSON TRIAL...
TODAY IN THE O.J. SIMPSON TRIAL...
CLICK
CLICK
CLICK
CLICK
CLICK
CLICK
TODAY IN THE O.J. SIMPSON TRIAL...
TODAY IN THE O.J. SIMPSON

57 CHANNELS AND ONE THING ON.
IN OTHER NEWS: **YESTERDAY** IN THE O.J. SIMPSON TRIAL...
AMEND

SEE WHAT HAPPENS WHEN YOU MAKE ME EAT SPINACH?!
JASON, IF YOU ORDER ONE MORE THING FROM THAT STUPID NOVELTY CATALOG...
A
AMEND

FoxTrot
BILL AMEND

MOM, IS IT OK IF I STAY OVER AT NICOLE'S?
PAIGE, NO.

YOU HAVEN'T FINISHED YOUR HOMEWORK... YOUR ROOM IS A MESS... YOU PROMISED YOU'D HELP ME WITH DINNER...

BESIDES, TONIGHT IS A SCHOOL NIGHT.
AMEND

ACTUALLY, I MEANT FOR THE WEEK.
THE WEEK??
GUESS WHAT MOVIE OPENS IN 5,526 MINUTES.

THAT'S ONE DOG-EARRED MAGAZINE.
IT'S THE CINEMAFANGIQUE "STAR TREK: GENERATIONS" PREVIEW ISSUE. I READ IT EVERY DAY AFTER SCHOOL.

IT'S GOT ALL THESE AMAZING BEHIND-THE-SCENES PHOTOS! HERE'S BRENT "DATA" SPINER GETTING HIS HAIR COMBED... HERE'S WORF SITTING IN BEVERLY CRUSHER'S DIRECTOR'S CHAIR... HERE'S PATRICK STEWART EATING A BAGEL BETWEEN SHOTS... I THINK IT'S POPPYSEED.

ISN'T THIS JUST THE COOLEST STUFF YOU'VE EVER SEEN IN YOUR LIFE, DAD?! ISN'T IT?! ISN'T IT?! ISN'T IT?!

I BELIEVE WHAT WE HAVE HERE IS A "STAR TREK: GENERATIONS" GAP.
HERE'S WILLIAM SHATNER TYING HIS SHOES...
AMEND

PETER! PETER! I DID IT!
SPATS ILLUSTRATED

I MEMORIZED THE ENTIRE KLINGON DICTIONARY! 191 PAGES AND I KNOW IT ALL! I'M GONNA BE THE BEST KLINGON IN THE THEATER FRIDAY, I KNOW IT!

ASK ME SOMETHING! ANYTHING! I KNOW ALL 1,400 WORDS!

WHY??
"QATLH." C'MON-GIMME SOMETHING HARD...
AMEND

MOM, HURRY UP! I DON'T WANT TO BE LATE!

EVERYBODY IN THE UNIVERSE IS GOING TO WANT TO SEE THIS "STAR TREK" MOVIE! IT'S PROBABLY SOLD-OUT ALREADY!

I TOLD MARCUS WE'D PICK HIM UP 10 MINUTES AGO! I'VE GOT YOUR CAR KEYS RIGHT HERE!
JASON, THIS MOVIE DOESN'T OPEN UNTIL TOMORROW.
AMEND

OOPS–I NEARLY FORGOT MY SLEEPING BAG.
IT'S AMAZING TO ME, JASON, HOW CUTE YOU WERE AS AN INFANT...

CAN I HELP YOU?
I AM KLINGON! I WANT A LARGE TUB OF NARENDIAN GAGH-WORMS!
Theaters 1+2

RAW! WITH EXTRA GAGH BLOOD! AND THEY HAD BETTER BE WIGGLING!

LOOK, KID, IT'S BEEN A REALLY LONG DAY...
OK, GIMME A MEDIUM POPCORN.
Theaters 3+4

WHY CAN'T WE JUST SHOW ART FLICKS?
DO YOUR REPLICATORS MAKE DECENT NACHOS?
Theaters 5-20
AMEND

GREAT. THE MOVIE EVENT OF A LIFETIME AND WE'RE STUCK BEHIND A COUPLE OF "HOMNS."
DID YOU BRING YOUR PHASER?
AMEND

FoxTrot
BILL AMEND

MOM, CAN I MAKE DINNER SOMETIME THIS WEEK?
SURE.

HOW 'BOUT THURSDAY?
FINE.

THIS'LL BE FUN. I'VE NEVER COOKED A TURKEY BEFORE.
PAIGE, DON'T MAKE TURKEY —WE'RE HAVING IT FOR THANKSGI···
AMEND

TOO LATE! YOU SAID YES!
GIVE ME THAT COOKBOOK!

THIS IS GOING TO BE THE MOST AMAZING THANKS-GIVING DINNER THIS FAM-ILY HAS EVER EXPERIENCED!

I'M GOING TO COOK OURS THE EXACT SAME WAY MARTHA STEWART COOKS HERS.
MARTHA STEWART'S THANKSGIVING

I'LL NEED A NEW WARDROBE.
THE AMAZEMENT BEGINS.
AMEND

PAIGE, WHAT ARE YOU DOING?
I'M DECORATING THE HOUSE FOR THANKSGIVING.
HARPER'S

I GATHERED A BUNCH OF LEAVES FROM THE YARD. I THOUGHT I'D MAKE A NICE CENTERPIECE, À LA MARTHA STEWART.
PAIGE, THOSE LEAVES ARE PROBABLY CRAWLING WITH BUGS.
AMEND

AIEEE!
HARPER'S

PAIGE, SWEETIE, THANKSGIVING IS ENOUGH WORK WITH-OUT YOUR ASSISTANCE.
EEK! NOW THE BUGS ARE ON THE FLOOR!
CRUNCH CRUNCH CRUNCH

THE COOKBOOK SAID TO CLEAN THE TURKEY... THE OVEN HAD A "CLEAN" BUTTON...
WHEN'S DINNER? WE'RE STARVED.
A
AMEND

SO WHAT DO YOU THINK OF MY PUMPKIN PIE?
MMM...

"MMM"?? REALLY??
MMM...

YOU'RE NOT JUST SAYING THAT TO BE NICE?
MMM... MMM... MMM...

HEY, EVERYONE– DADDY LIKES MY PIE!
MMM... YYY... JAWWW... ISSS... GLUUUED... SHHHUT...
AMEND

SWEETIE, WHAT'S WRONG?
MOTHER, I'M SORRY MY DINNER WAS SUCH A MESS.
Atlantic

IT WASN'T A MESS.
ARE YOU KIDDING?! THE TURKEY WAS LIKE CHARCOAL, THE GRAVY WAS A SOLID MASS, AND THE PUMPKIN PIE PULLED OUT TWO OF DADDY'S FILLINGS!

REALLY, IT WASN'T A MESS.
IT WAS **TOO**!
AMEND

LOOK, PAIGE, COMPARED TO WHAT YOU LEFT FOR ME IN THE KITCHEN...
WELL, THAT GOES **BEYOND** "MESS"...

FoxTrot
BILL AMEND

IT'S SNOWING! IT'S SNOWING!

THEY'RE GOING TO CANCEL SCHOOL! THEY'RE GOING TO CANCEL SCHOOL!

I SUPPOSE I SHOULD BE FLATTERED THAT THE UNIVERSE HAS IT OUT FOR ME.
YIPPEE! SCHOOL'S NOT CANCELED!
AMEND

I DON'T GET IT.
WHAT?
CLICK CLICK CLICK

I PICKED UP THIS RUBIK'S CUBE AT THE NEIGHBOR'S GARAGE SALE. APPARENTLY THIS WAS LIKE THE PUZZLE OF THE 1980s.
IT WAS, BELIEVE ME.

IT'S MIND-BOGGLING. I JUST CAN'T FIGURE IT OUT.
HOW TO DO IT?
CLICK CLICK CLICK

HOW PEOPLE COULD THINK THIS WAS HARD.
SPEAKING OF THINGS MIND-BOGGLING...
AMEND

OOF!

UGGH!

MAN!

YOU KNOW, YOU COULD MAKE YOUR BAG LUNCHES SMALLER...
CAN YOU GIVE ME A HAND WITH THE DOOR?
AMEND

AMEND
YOU KNOW, FOR SOMEONE WHO CLAIMS TO BE SO GOOD AT PHYSICS...
UM, WE'VE GOT SPACKLE, RIGHT?

PLEASE CAN I GO SEE "INTERVIEW WITH THE VAMPIRE"??
NO.

PLEEEASE CAN I GO SEE "INTERVIEW WITH THE VAMPIRE"??
NO.

WAAAAAAAAAA! WHY NOT??
BECAUSE THE MOVIE IS RATED "R"!

C'MON—I'M MATURE ENOUGH...
JASON, FETCH ME THAT SPONGE.
AMEND

AMEND

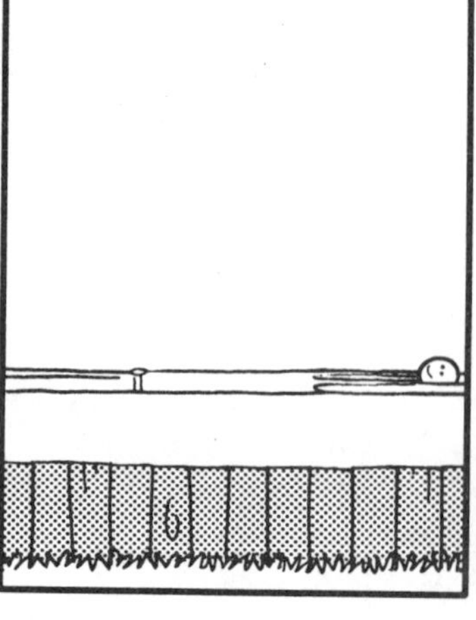

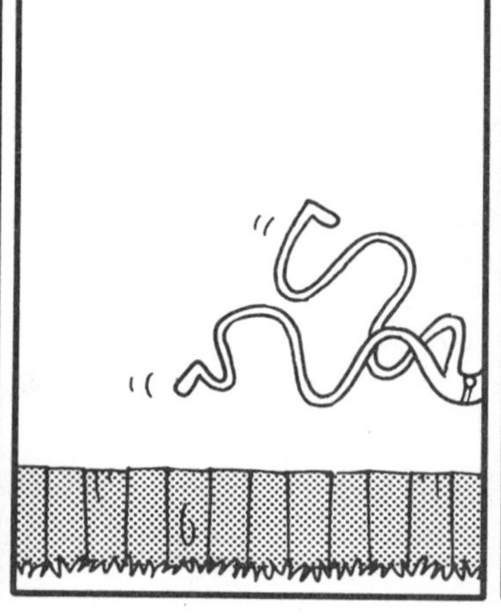

I DIDN'T LET GO ON PURPOSE, I SWEAR!
I THINK STRETCH ARMSTRONG MAY BE A TOY BEST PLAYED WITH ALONE.

FoxTrot

BILL AMEND

MONDAY NIGHT FOOTBALL...
Toridos

IN THE MIDDLE OF A SNOWSTORM... A BEER IN ONE HAND... CHIPS IN THE OTHER...
Toridos
AMEND

WHAT MORE COULD YOU ASK FOR?
Toridos

INTACT POWER LINES?
AAAA!

LOOK AT THIS MAIL!...

CATALOG, CATALOG, CATALOG, FLIER, CATALOG, CATALOG, CATALOG...
Meiman Narcus

HOW DO WE GET ON THESE MAILING LISTS?!
AMEND

PETER, GET OFF THE PHONE!
AND WHY IS OUR VISA BILL TWO INCHES THICK?

AMEND

NOW THEN, WHO TO PIN THIS ON?
JASON, DON'T YOU EVER HAVE HOMEWORK??

A SUBSTITUTE TEACHER IN ENGLISH...
Cashier

MARY BEAUTIFUL BRUSHING AGAINST US IN THE HALL...
AMEND

TACOS FOR LUNCH...

CLEARLY, THERE IS A GOD.
AT LEAST UNTIL THE TRIG TEST.

Beep Beep
I'VE GOT TO START COMING HOME AFTER DARK.
AMEND

WHAT ARE YOU DOING?
OH, WITH THE HOLIDAYS COMING UP, I THOUGHT I'D KNIT MYSELF A LITTLE SOMETHING.

MOM, HERE'S AN ADDENDUM TO MY CHRISTMAS LIST.
MOM, WERE THE COOKIES SUPPOSED TO TURN BLACK LIKE THIS?
MOM, DON'T TELL ME THIS WAS ALL THE EGGNOG YOU BOUGHT.

UM, STRAIT-JACKETS HAVE LONGER SLEEVES.
YOU **LAUGH**..
AMEND

FoxTrot

BILL AMEND

THYME

YOU MIGHT WANT TO ASK SANTA TO REPLACE A FEW OLD-GROWTH FORESTS WHILE YOU'RE AT IT.
PRINTZZZZ
PRINTZZZZ
PRINTZZZZ
PRINTZZZZ
I JUST HOPE HE CAN READ THIS LIST IN TWO WEEKS.
AMEND

I DON'T KNOW WHAT TO GET YOUR BROTHER JASON FOR CHRISTMAS.

THERE ARE JUST TOO MANY TOYS, TOO MANY VIDEO GAMES TO CHOOSE FROM!

IT'S UNREAL.
DIDN'T HE MAKE A LIST?

I'M TALKING ABOUT HIS LIST.
YOU COULD BUY THE KID SOME SEDATIVES.
AMEND

BUILDING A SNOWMAN?
NOT JUST ANY SNOWMAN.

THIS WILL BE THE BIGGEST, THE HUGEST, THE MOST COLOSSAL SNOWMAN THE WORLD HAS EVER SEEN!
AMEND

HE DOESN'T LOOK VERY BIG.
THIS IS ONE OF HIS MOLECULES.

AH, SILLY ME.
CAN YOU TELL MOM I MIGHT BE A LITTLE LATE FOR DINNER?

Let Set A represent all three-letter words.
Let Set B represent all four-letter words.
Math
Jason Fox

Let Set C represent all words containing two vowels.
Math
Jason Fox
AMEND
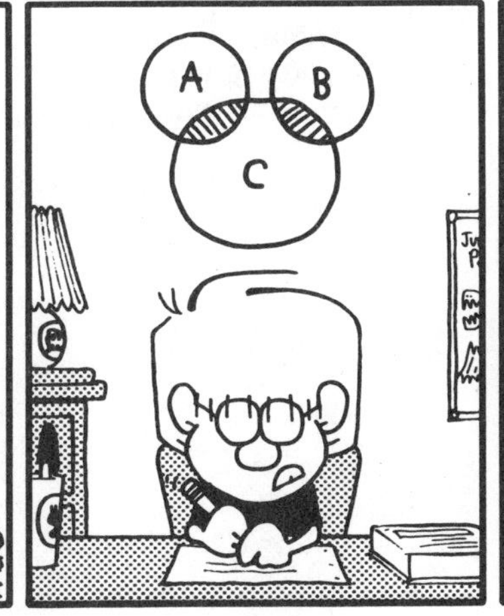
A
B
C

I HATE THESE MICKEY MOUSE PROBLEMS.

IT'S RIDICULOUS!

HOW AM I SUPPOSED TO DO ALL THIS HOMEWORK LESS THAN TWO WEEKS BEFORE CHRISTMAS?!

THERE ARE JUST TOO MANY DISTRACTIONS! HOW AM I SUPPOSED TO STAY FOCUSED?! HOW AM I SUPPOSED TO GET MOTIVATED?! HOW AM I SUPPOSED TO EVEN THINK ABOUT SCHOOLWORK?!

LET ME GET THIS STRAIGHT – YOU WANT ME TO JUST STAND HERE AND GLARE...
IF YOU DON'T MIND.

HEY, PAIGE, WANNA PLAY BLACKJACK?
OK.

I'LL DEAL. (FLIP FLIP FLIP FLIP) YOU SHOW A FOUR, I SHOW A SEVEN.
HIT ME.

I'M SORRY – MY HEARING MUST BE GOING. WHAT WAS THAT?
I SAID HIT ME.
AMEND

NOW THAT'S WHAT I CALL A CARD GAME.
HEY, JASON, WANNA PLAY WAR?

JASON, I APPRECIATE YOUR DESIRE TO HELP DECORATE THE TREE THIS YEAR.

IT'S A FAMILY TRADITION AND IT WARMS MY HEART TO SEE YOU SO EAGERLY JOINING IN.
AMEND

BUT SWEETIE...
I KNEW THERE'D BE A "BUT"...

DON'T YOU THINK PLASTIC SKELETONS ARE MORE APPRO-PRIATE FOR HALLOWEEN?
BUT THEY GLOW IN THE DARK! YOU WON'T HAVE TO MESS WITH LIGHTS!

FoxTrot
BILL AMEND

WELL, ANDY, YOU'LL BE PLEASED TO KNOW I'M NOT GOING TO GO CRAZY DECORATING THE HOUSE THIS CHRISTMAS.

EVERY YEAR I TRY TO OUTDO THE NEIGHBORS, AND EVERY YEAR I END UP NEARLY ELEC-TROCUTING MYSELF IN THE PROCESS. THERE COMES A POINT WHERE A MAN JUST HAS TO RECOGNIZE HIS OWN LIMITATIONS.

SO... NO MORE FANCY LIGHTING SCHEMES FOR THIS HOMEOWNER. NO SIRREE.
WHY, ROGER, I DO BELIEVE YOU'RE SHOWING SIGNS OF SANITY IN YOUR OLD AGE.
AMEND

I'M LETTING JASON DO IT.
AS USUAL, I SPOKE TOO SOON.
I ASSUME YOU'D LIKE TO KEEP THE COST UNDER FIVE FIGURES, IF POSSIBLE.

WHAT'S WITH ALL THE MAGAZINES?
I'M TRYING TO FIGURE OUT HOW I WANT TO LIGHT OUR HOUSE FOR CHRISTMAS.
Nonde Cast

I'M GOING THROUGH THESE TRAVEL MAGAZINES LOOKING FOR INSPIRATIONAL PHOTOS.
Nonde Cast

OF COZY NEW ENGLAND HAMLETS?
OF THE LAS VEGAS STRIP.
Nonde Cast

AH, TO BE THE FIRST HOUSE ON OUR BLOCK WITH NEON.
MOVING NEON.
AMEND

WHAT ARE YOU DOING?
DRAWING UP PRELIMINARY SKETCHES OF HOW I'M GOING TO DECORATE OUR YARD FOR CHRISTMAS.
RUFFLES

IT'S IMPORTANT TO BEGIN WITH A UNIFYING THEME TO TIE EVERYTHING TOGETHER, BUT I CAN'T DECIDE WHICH IDEA I LIKE BEST.

I STARTED OFF THINKING I'D DO A STANDARD SANTA'S VILLAGE, BUT THEN I THOUGHT OF DOING ONE A BIT MORE PIRATE-ORIENTED. THEN I HAD THIS GREAT IDEA: A **JURASSIC** CHRISTMAS. WHAT DO YOU THINK?

I THINK THESE PENS' FUMES MUST PACK QUITE A WALLOP.
STILL, I LIKE THE IDEA OF SANTA SAYING YO HO HO..
AMEND

WHAT DO YOU NEED A TAPE MEASURE FOR?
I'M TRYING TO FIGURE OUT HOW MANY OUTDOOR CHRISTMAS LIGHTS WE'LL NEED.
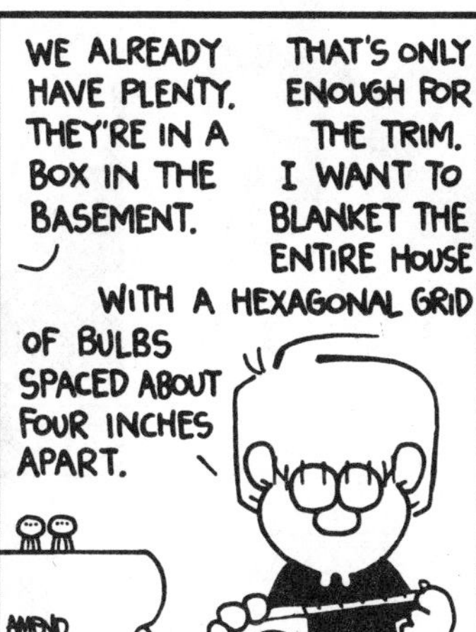
WE ALREADY HAVE PLENTY. THEY'RE IN A BOX IN THE BASEMENT.
THAT'S ONLY ENOUGH FOR THE TRIM. I WANT TO BLANKET THE ENTIRE HOUSE WITH A HEXAGONAL GRID OF BULBS SPACED ABOUT FOUR INCHES APART.
AMEND

OUT OF CURIOSITY, WHAT'S THE FLASH POINT OF WOOD SIDING?

WHAT DO YOU NEED ASPIRIN FOR?
I'LL TELL YOU AFTER THEY KICK IN.

MOM, CAN I BUY TWO MORE STRINGS OF OUTDOOR LIGHTS? PLEEEASE?
JASON, WE'VE GOT MORE THAN ENOUGH LIGHTS AS IT IS.

BUT I WANT TO SPELL OUT A HOLIDAY MESSAGE UP ON THE ROOF FOR PASSING AIRPLANES.
WHAT MESSAGE?

"HAVE FUN FINDING YOUR LUGGAGE AND MAKING CONNECTIONS IN THIS WEATHER! HA HA HA!"

RIGHT NOW I'VE ONLY GOT ENOUGH FOR ONE "HA."
YOU KNOW HOW, OCCASIONALLY, YOU READ ABOUT AN AIRPLANE DUMPING ITS FUEL?...
AMEND

I FEEL LIKE SUCH A FAILURE.
HOW'S THAT?

I SPENT ALL WEEK PLANNING TO DECORATE THE OUTSIDE OF OUR HOUSE LIKE NEVER BEFORE! I WAS GOING TO HAVE LASERS, FOG, NEON, A VELOCIRAPTOR-DRIVEN SANTA SLEIGH, AN AUDIO-ANIMATRONIC SNOWMAN SHOW AND A 200-WATT SOUND SYSTEM BLASTING "JINGLE BELL ROCK" 24 HOURS A DAY!

BUT NOW IT'S CHRISTMAS EVE AND I'VE RUN OUT OF TIME...
THYME

...TO GET THE SOUND SYSTEM INSTALLED.
MY QUESTION IS, DID YOU DECORATE LIKE NEVER AGAIN?
JASON, YOUR SNOWMEN ARE ON FIRE!
AMEND

FoxTrot
BILL AMEND

CAN IT BE?!

Rip Rip Rip Rip Rip Rip Rip Rip Rip Rip

YAAAAA! A "STREET KOMBAT II" GAME CARTRIDGE!
Power Turtles

THIS IS THE ONE I REALLY WANTED! OH, THANK YOU, SANTA! THANK YOU! THANK YOU!

VIDGAMER DIGEST GAVE THIS CARTRIDGE ITS HIGHEST RATING EVER! IT'S SUPPOSED TO BE AMAZING!

IN THIS ONE ROUND, YOU GET TO FIGHT EACH OTHER WITH RUSTY CHAINSAWS! MARCUS SAYS THEY USED SGI WORK-STATIONS TO REN-DER THE BLOOD SPLATTERS IN 3-D!

FOR SIX MONTHS, ALL I'VE DREAMED ABOUT IS OWNING THIS VIDEO GAME CARTRIDGE AND NOW I'VE GOT IT! I'M THE HAPPIEST KID ALIVE!

THIS IS WHAT CHRISTMAS IS ALL ABOUT.

I MEAN, YOU KNOW, APART FROM ALL THAT OTHER STUFF.

JASON AND I WILL BE AT CHURCH IF ANYONE NEEDS US.
IN YOUR PAJAMAS??
WHAT MAKES YOU THINK THEY'RE EVEN OPEN TODAY?
AMEND

WHAT ARE YOU DOING?
TRYING TO COME UP WITH A GOOD NEW YEAR'S RESOLUTION.

I WANT SOMETHING SIGNIFICANT, YET DOABLE. I TAKE THESE VOWS SERIOUSLY.

WHAT'D YOU RESOLVE LAST YEAR?
NOT TO PROCRASTINATE SO MUCH.
AMEND

AHH.
OH, WHAT THE HECK. I STILL HAVE FIVE DAYS TO DO THIS.

HAVE **YOU** THOUGHT OF A NEW YEAR'S RESOLUTION?
ACTUALLY, YES, I HAVE.

I'M RESOLVING TO BE YOUR NEW BEST FRIEND. BEGINNING SUNDAY, WE'LL BE INSEPARABLE. WHEN YOU WATCH TV, **I'LL** WATCH TV. WHEN YOU GO TO THE MALL, **I'LL** GO TO THE MALL.

IF YOU EVEN **THINK** OF FOLLOWING ME TO THE MALL...
...AND WHEN YOU SAY THINGS LIKE THAT, I'LL JUST SAY, "I LOVE YOU, SIS."
AMEND

AAAAAAAAAAAA!
I THOUGHT YOUR RESOLUTION WAS TO DRIVE PAIGE NUTS.
SO I STARTED A LITTLE EARLY.
Next Issue:
Illustrated Sports

PETER, DO YOU MAKE NEW YEAR'S RESOLUTIONS?
NOPE.

HOW COME?
IT JUST SEEMS KINDA POINTLESS. YOU START OUT WITH ALL THESE HIGH HOPES AND EXPECTATIONS, BUT THEN EVENTUALLY REALITY SETS IN AND IT ALL GOES OUT THE WINDOW.

THEN YOU FEEL DEPRESSED UNTIL THE **NEXT** YEAR, WHEN YOU BASICALLY DO THE EXACT SAME THING ALL OVER AGAIN. IT'S AN ENDLESS CYCLE OF FAILURE. WHY BOTHER?!
AMEND

THIS FROM A DIE-HARD RED SOX FAN.
HEY, THEY'RE WINNING IT **ALL** THIS YEAR– YOU **WATCH**...

YOUR MOTHER SAYS YOU'RE LOOKING FOR A GOOD NEW YEAR'S RESOLUTION.
CHESS PIECES
Verlon
Fourteen

HOW ABOUT PLEDGING TO PLAY CHESS WITH YOUR OLD MAN EVERY ONCE IN A WHILE?
CHESS PIECES

WHADDYA SAY?
CHESS PIECES
Levron
Fourteen

I SAID "CHESS," NOT "FRISBEE"!...
AMEND

WELL, I'VE GOT MY NEW YEAR'S RESOLUTION ALL READY TO GO.
OH? WHAT IS IT?

TO BE MORE DECISIVE!... CONFIDENT!... SURE!... TO KNOW WHAT I WANT AND GO FULL STEAM AHEAD!
AMEND

DOES THAT SOUND STUPID? IF IT DOES, I CAN CHANGE IT...
LET'S BACK THOSE STEAM ENGINES UP FOR A SECOND...

New Year's Resolution
I, Paige Fox, promise to keep my temper under control.

PAIGE, I THINK QUINCY CHEWED UP ONE OF YOUR SWEATERS.
AMEND

I THINK IT WAS THAT NICE ONE YOU BOUGHT WITH ALL OF YOUR CHRISTMAS MONEY.

will try
promise
CAN YOU GRAB THE KLEENEX? QUINCY'S THROWING UP ON YOUR BED.

FoxTrot
BILL AMEND

I CAN'T BELIEVE TODAY'S REALLY A HOLIDAY.

I CAN'T BELIEVE I REALLY DON'T HAVE TO GO TO WORK.

MOM! JASON'S SHOOTING FROOT LOOPS OUT OF HIS NOSE!
AMEND

BLASTED CALENDAR.
JASON, GIVE ME THAT CEREAL!
PAIGE STARTED IT.
DID NOT!
DID TOO.
OW!

MOM, CAN I TAKE THE CAR TO DENISE'S HOUSE? SHE INVITED ME OVER FOR LUNCH.

THAT'S FINE. WHEN WILL YOU BE HOME?
PROBABLY SOMETIME AROUND 2:00.
AMEND

AHEM.
...P.M.

HAVE FUN.
THE CURSE OF THE PARANOID MOTHER...

UM, MOM? MY SOUP KINDA EXPLODED IN THE MICROWAVE.
HOW DID THAT HAPPEN?!

I DON'T KNOW.
DID YOU FOLLOW THE INSTRUCTIONS?
AMEND

I FORGET.
WELL, LET'S FIND OUT. WHERE'S THE CAN?

I TOLD YOU, IT EXPLODED.
PAIGE, DIDN'T WE GO THROUGH THIS WITH OUR FIRST MICROWAVE?

WHAT ARE YOU DOING?
WRITING A COMPUTER PROGRAM TO DETERMINE THE IDEAL SNOWBALL.

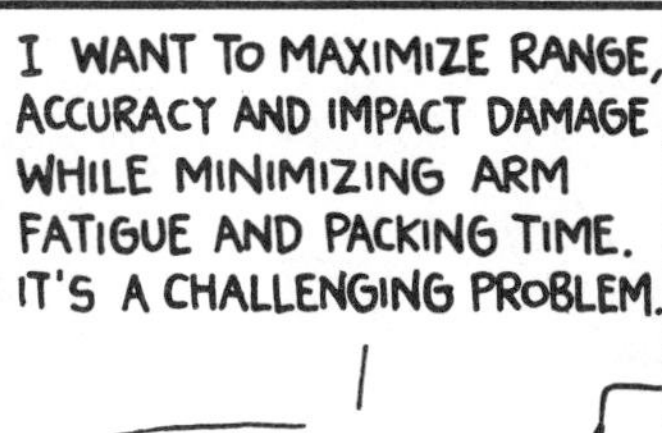
I WANT TO MAXIMIZE RANGE, ACCURACY AND IMPACT DAMAGE WHILE MINIMIZING ARM FATIGUE AND PACKING TIME. IT'S A CHALLENGING PROBLEM.

STILL, KNOWING THE PERFECT SIZE, SHAPE AND MASS IS JUST THE SORT OF EDGE I CAN EXPLOIT THE NEXT TIME PAIGE COMES NEAR MY SNOW FORT. HEE HEE HEE.

MEANTIME IT'S SPRING...
GOOD POINT. I PROBABLY SHOULD ACCOUNT FOR AIR TEMPERATURE.
AMEND

I'M TELLING YOU, MOM, "THE X-FILES" IS THE COOLEST SHOW ON TV.

NOT JUST ONCE IN A WHILE, EITHER. EVERY EPISODE IS COOL, START TO FINISH. TOTALLY. FULLY. BIG-TIME.

AND I KNOW COOL.
ARE THESE LT. WORF UNDERPANTS YOURS?
AMEND

STEVE YOUNG FADES BACK TO PASS!

HE SPOTS AN OPEN JERRY RICE STREAKING DOWNFIELD!

ACTUALLY, DAD, MAYBE WE SHOULD JUST STICK TO HANDOFFS.
(OOF) STUPID POSTSEASON...
AMEND

FoxTrot

BILL AMEND

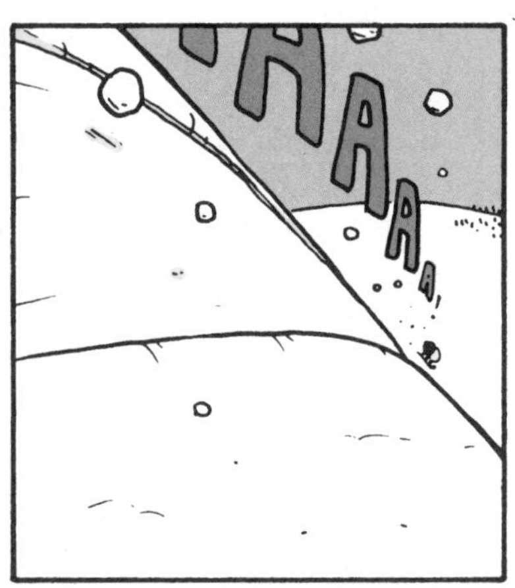

JASON MUST HAVE SOME BIG HOMEWORK ASSIGNMENT DUE TOMORROW.
WHY DO YOU SAY THAT?

HE'S HAD HIS NOSE BURIED IN EITHER A DICTIONARY OR A THESAURUS FOR MOST OF THE EVENING.

I MEAN, I CAN'T IMAGINE A NORMAL KID JUST DOING THAT FOR **FUN**.

THE KEY WORD, ROGER, IS "**NORMAL**."
HAS ANYONE EVER TOLD YOU THAT YOUR CORPULENCE IS DOWNRIGHT BROBDINGNAGIAN?
AMEND

DR. TING?
YES, PAIGE?

ABOUT FRIDAY'S TEST— DOES IT COVER ALL OF CHAPTER FOUR AND PART OF CHAPTER FIVE, OR PART OF CHAPTER FOUR AND ALL OF CHAPTER FIVE?
AMEND

HI, BOBBY! I LIKE YOUR SWEATER!
IT COVERS CHAPTERS 11 AND 12.

I'M SORRY, WHAT WAS THAT?
BY THE WAY, THE TEST IS ON THURSDAY.

I AM SO FULL.

I DEFINITELY ATE TOO MUCH.

I THINK I'M GOING TO EXPLODE.

SO WHAT'S FOR DESSERT?
AMEND

HEY, MOM, LOOK! I GOT AN "A-" ON MY HISTORY ASSIGNMENT!
PETER, GOOD FOR YOU!

WE HAD TO LIST 10 GREAT AMERICANS AND WRITE A PARAGRAPH ABOUT EACH ONE.

I HAD JEFFERSON, FRANKLIN, KING, LINCOLN... IT WAS THE PERFECT LIST.
SO WHY AN A-MINUS?

APPARENTLY "GREAT" IS A RELATIVE TERM.
YOU INCLUDED YOURSELF?!
AMEND

POW!

UM, WITHOUT ADMITTING ANYTHING, I BELIEVE THAT'S MY MITTEN.
SUCH PRETTY LITTLE TEETH...
AMEND

WHY ARE YOU IN YOUR PAJAMAS?
I'M GOING TO BED.

NOW?!
I KNOW IT'S EARLY, BUT I FIGURE THE SOONER I GO TO BED, THE SOONER IT'LL BE TOMORROW MORNING. AND WE ALL KNOW WHAT TOMORROW IS...

SUPER BOWL SUNDAY!

AT LEAST EAT SOME LUNCH FIRST.
I JUST WISH I WERE TIRED.
AMEND

FoxTrot
BILL AMEND

RUNNING SHOES...

OVERCOAT...

IGUANA.

MOTH-ERRR!
HOW TO REALLY DRESS FOR SUCCESS.
AMEND

GREETINGS. I AM IGUANOMAN.
JASON, YOU ARE SO WEIRD.

I COME FROM A GALAXY FAR, FAR AWAY, BUT I SEEM TO HAVE MADE A WRONG TURN SOMEWHERE.

COULD YOU POSSIBLY DIRECT ME TO THE PLANET EARTH?
THIS IS EARTH, YOU GEEK!
AMEND

RIGHT. AND I SUPPOSE YOU'RE GOING TO TELL ME YOU'RE HUMAN.
ACTUALLY, I'M ON THE VERGE OF GOING APE.

GREETINGS, EARTHLING. WHAT'S FOR DINNER?
ZITI NEFERTITI.

WHAT'S THAT?
OH, JUST A LITTLE SOMETHING I MADE UP. IT'S PASTA TUBES STUFFED WITH MASHED EGGPLANT AND GREEN OLIVES.

I WAS AFRAID OF THIS. MY DIGESTIVE TRACT IS INCOMPATIBLE WITH YOUR HUMANOID DIET. I WILL REQUIRE ALTERNATIVE SUSTENANCE.
SUCH AS?
AMEND

I BELIEVE YOU EARTHLINGS CALL THEM "HO HO'S."
JASON, MUST WE GO THROUGH THIS EVERY OTHER DAY?

JASON, WILL YOU GET **LOST**?!
I TOLD YOU, I AM NOT JASON. I AM IGUANOMAN.

FINE. IGUANOMAN, WILL YOU GET **LOST**?!
YOUR TONE OF DISRESPECT IS A SURE WAY TO LAND YOURSELF A SLAVE JOB IN ONE OF MY PLANET'S CRICKET MINES. I DEMAND AN APOLOGY.
AMEND

AND THOSE NACHOS.

DOES MOLTEN CHEESE STAIN?
ORDINARILY, I'D ASK "HOW"...

WELL, WELL, WHAT HAVE WE HERE?
I AM IGUANOMAN. YOU MUST BE THE ONE THEY CALL "DAD."

THAT WOULD BE ME.
I HAVE TRAVELED LIGHT-YEARS THROUGH SPACE TO BRING YOU A MESSAGE FROM MY SUPREME COMMANDER, IGUANIUS THE ALMIGHTY.
AMEND
AND WHAT MIGHT THAT MESSAGE BE?
"INCREASE JASON FOX'S ALLOWANCE OR WE WILL DESTROY YOUR PLANET."

SON, WOULD YOU **LIKE** YOUR FATHER TO START HITTING BARS ON THE WAY HOME FROM WORK?
NOW, GIVEN THAT THE EARTH IS PROBABLY WORTH A FEW QUADRILLION DOLLARS...

STUPID PHYSICS.
WHY DO YOU SAY THAT?

I WANT TO GO BACK TO MY PLANET FOR LUNCH, BUT TRAVELING AT THE SPEEDS I DO, RELATIVITY THEORY TELLS ME THAT YOU ALL WILL HAVE AGED THOUSANDS OF YEARS BY THE TIME I RETURN. YOU'LL BE NOTHING BUT DUST BY THEN.

WHAT A PITY.
THAT WE WON'T MEET AGAIN?
AMEND

THAT I WON'T GET TO WATCH YOU SHRIVEL UP.
JASON, I WOULDN'T BE SO SURE **YOU'LL** BE OUTLIVING **ME**...

FoxTrot

BILL AMEND

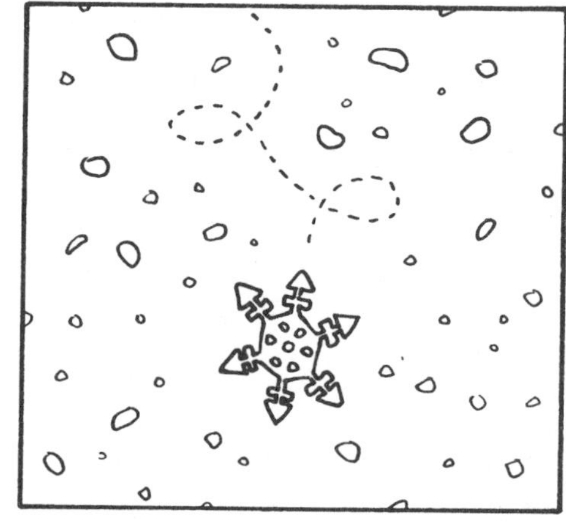

OW!

YOU KNOW HOW THEY SAY NO TWO SNOWFLAKES ARE ALIKE?

IS THIS SOMETHING THEY CAN PROVE, OR IS IT JUST SOME OLD WIVES' TALE KIND OF THING?

I MEAN, THERE MUST BE TRILLIONS OF SNOWFLAKES FALLING AROUND THE WORLD RIGHT NOW.

AND ARE YOU ALLOWED TO COMPARE PRESENT SNOWFLAKES WITH PAST ONES? BECAUSE THEN YOU'D HAVE TO INCLUDE ALL THE ZILLIONS OF SNOWFLAKES THAT HAVE FALLEN IN THE EARTH'S 4.6 BILLION-YEAR HISTORY.
THAT'S A LOT.

AND WHAT ABOUT SNOWFLAKES THAT MIGHT FALL ON OTHER PLANETS? DO WE GET TO COMPARE THOSE TOO? EVENTUALLY THERE'D HAVE TO BE DUPLICATES!

OF COURSE, IF THEY'RE TALKING ABOUT BEING THE SAME RIGHT DOWN TO EACH ATOM, THE HEISENBERG UNCERTAINTY PRINCIPLE WOULD MAKE EXACT COMPARISONS CONVENIENTLY IMPOSSIBLE.

HMMM...
AMEND

I WONDER IF PHILOSOPHERS DIE MORE OFTEN IN THE WINTER.
AND WHAT ABOUT MAN-MADE SNOWFLAKES?

ANDY, I'VE GOT A LOT OF WORK ON MY DESK I NEED TO CATCH UP ON.

I'D LIKE TO STAY HERE AT THE OFFICE A WHILE LONGER, IF THAT'S OK.
WHEN WILL YOU BE HOME?
AMEND

PROBABLY AROUND 9:00.
ROGER, THIS IS THE THIRD STRAIGHT WEEK YOU'VE DONE THIS.

SINCE WHEN ARE MONDAYS SO AWFUL?
"MELROSE"!
"VOYAGER"!
"MELROSE"!
"VOYAGER"!
"MELROSE"!
LET GO!
OW!

IT'S UNBELIEVABLE HOW MUCH HOMEWORK I HAVE TO DO TONIGHT!

I CAN'T REMEMBER THE LAST TIME I HAD THIS MANY THINGS DUE!

I DON'T KNOW WHAT ALL MY TEACHERS WERE THINKING!
IN THAT CASE, SWEETIE, WHY DON'T I DO THE DISHES?
AMEND

I THOUGHT YOU HAD NO HOMEWORK...
IT'S ALL IN HOW YOU SAY IT.
MRI SPECS

JASON WAS SO DARLING THIS MORNING.
OH?

HE WANTED TO KNOW IF HE COULD BRING THAT CUTE PICTURE OF PAIGE TO SCHOOL FOR HIS CLASSMATES TO SEE.
I WONDER WHAT FOR.
AMEND

I ASSUME BECAUSE HE WANTS TO SHOW OFF HIS SISTER. WHAT OTHER REASON COULD THERE BE?

...AND TO CONCLUDE MY REPORT, I OFFER PHOTOGRAPHIC PROOF OF THE SASQUATCH!
THANK YOU, JASON. YOU CAN SIT DOWN NOW.

Farmer Bob's field measures 150 yards by 250 yards.
Math
Paige Fox

He wants to use 60 percent of his land for growing brussels sprouts, 30 percent for lima beans, and 10 percent for cauliflower.
Math
Paige Fox

What is the square footage he'll need to allocate for each crop?
AMEND

LIKE I'M REALLY GONNA LIFT A FINGER TO HELP THIS GUY.

GLUG
GLUG
GLUG
GLUG
GLUG
AMEND

WHERE'S PAIGE?? WHERE'S PAIGE?? WHERE'S PAIGE??
UPSTAIRS, I THINK.

BRAAAP!

TOO LATE. NEVER MIND.
PETER, WHY DON'T YOU GO UPSTAIRS ANYWAY.

PAIGE, YOU KNOW YOUR MOTHER PRETTY WELL. WHAT DO YOU THINK I SHOULD GET HER FOR VALENTINE'S DAY?
Fourteen

CHOCOLATES. ONE OF THOSE REALLY BIG, HEART-SHAPED BOXES. WITH LOTS OF COCONUT ONES.
AMEND

BUT YOUR MOTHER'S ON A DIET.
I'M NOT.

PETER, YOU KNOW YOUR MOTHER PRETTY WELL...
OK, FINE. FLOWERS AND CHOCOLATES.

FoxTrot

BILL AMEND

The Drama Club
Announces
Open Auditions For
ANTONY
and
CLEOPATRA
All this week 3pm
in the Auditorium

STRANGE... I SUDDENLY FEEL AS THOUGH I'M BEING TUGGED BY AN OVERWHELMING FORCE.

THAT'D BE ME SAYING WE'RE GONNA BE LATE FOR CLASS.
NO, NO - IT'S A **NEW** SORT OF TUGGING.
AMEND

HI. I'M HERE TO AUDITION FOR "ANTONY AND CLEOPATRA."
GREAT. HERE'S A COPY OF THE PLAY. WE'LL BE STARTING IN A MINUTE.

SAY, YOU LOOK REALLY FAMILIAR. HAVE WE MET?

DIDN'T I SEE YOU IN "STREETCAR" LAST SUMMER?

ACTUALLY, I TRY TO AVOID PUBLIC TRANS-PORTATION.
OOO - AN IMPROV TYPE. I **LIKE** THIS GIRL!
AMEND

UM, I'M NOT SURE WHAT PART I SHOULD BE TRYING OUT FOR.
DON'T WORRY ABOUT CASTING, PAIGE. THAT'S MY JOB.

YOU JUST READ THE LINES I'VE HIGHLIGHTED AND WE'LL FIGURE OUT WHERE TO PUT YOU.

"MY DEFECATION DOES BEGIN TO MAKE A BETTER LIFE. 'TIS PALTRY TO BE CAESAR."
AMEND

OOPS - I MEAN "DESOLATION."
THIS MIGHT BE A GOOD TIME TO MENTION THAT WE **ARE** ALSO LOOKING FOR STAGE HANDS.

STEVE SAYS HE SAW YOU AUDITIONING FOR SOME PLAY AFTER SCHOOL.
"ANTONY AND CLEOPATRA." SO?

DID YOU MAKE IT?
DON'T KNOW. THEY'LL ANNOUNCE ALL THE CASTING DECISIONS AT THE END OF THE WEEK.

MEANTIME, I CAN'T TELL YOU HOW SCARED I AM.
AMEND

THAT YOU WON'T GET A PART?
NO, THAT I ACTUALLY MIGHT.

YOU REALLY WANT ME TO PLAY CLEOPATRA?!
ABSOLUTELY, PAIGE. I THINK YOU'LL BE GREAT.

THIS IS INCREDIBLE! I NEVER WOULD HAVE DREAMED THIS WAS POSSIBLE!

ALL MY LIFE I'VE FELT JINXED! ALL MY LIFE I'VE FELT UNLUCKY! FINALLY, FINALLY, THAT'S ALL TURNED AROUND!
AMEND

SO WHO'S PLAYING ANTONY?
I BELIEVE YOU KNOW MORTON.
MY QUEEN...

YES, PAIGE?
FRITZ, I JUST NOTICED THAT THIS PLAY WAS WRITTEN BY SHAKESPEARE.

THE BARD HIMSELF.
IS IT OK IF I JUST USE THE CLIFFS NOTES?
Antony and Cleopatra
AMEND

THIS GIRL JUST KEEPS CRACKING ME UP!
NO, SERIOUSLY...

FoxTrot

BILL AMEND

MOM! MOM! I DID IT! I THOUGHT IT'D BE IMPOSSIBLE, BUT IT WASN'T!

SHAKESPEARE'S NOT SO TOUGH! SHAKESPEARE'S NOT SO HARD TO LEARN! IT TOOK A COUPLE WEEKS, BUT I'VE GOT THIS BABY DOWN COLD.

I'M GONNA WALK OUT ONTO THAT STAGE WITH MORE CONFIDENCE THAN YOU CAN IMAGINE.
YOU MEMORIZED ALL YOUR LINES?

I MEMORIZED MY ENTRANCE CUE.
PAIGE, THIS PLAY OPENS WHEN?
AMEND

SEE THIS TAPE ON THE FLOOR, PAIGE? THIS IS YOUR MARK.

WHEN YOU FIRST ENTER THE SCENE, I WANT YOU TO BE SURE TO HIT IT BEFORE YOU START SPEAKING.
GOTCHA.

OK, PEOPLE, LET'S TRY THIS AGAIN.
HUSH! HERE COMES ANTONY.
NOT HE; THE QUEEN.
WHAM! WHAM! WHAM! WHAM!

I MEANT STAND ON IT, PAIGE.
THAT WOULD MAKE MORE SENSE.
AMEND

ACT IV, SCENE XV.
HUH?

ACT IV, SCENE XV.
WHAT ARE YOU TALKING ABOUT?!

ACT IV, SCENE XV.
BLAH BLAH BLAH... "I AM DYING, -EGYPT, DYING"... BLAH BLAH BLAH... "I DARE NOT, DEAR"... BLAH BLAH BLAH... AACK! THEY KISS?!
Antony and Cleopatra
AMEND

NO, PAIGE, YOU CAN'T HAVE A STUNT DOUBLE.
LOOK, I'M NOT SUPPOSED TO DIE UNTIL ACT V...
ACT IV, SCENE XV...

OK, ANTONY, YOU'VE JUST BEEN TOLD THAT CLEOPATRA HAS KILLED HERSELF AND THE ANGUISH CAUSES YOU TO THROW YOURSELF UPON YOUR OWN SWORD.

AMEND

TELL YOU WHAT–LET'S USE YOUR DAGGER INSTEAD.
I THINK THAT WAS MY DAGGER.
ABOUT THIS PLAY BEING A TRAGEDY...

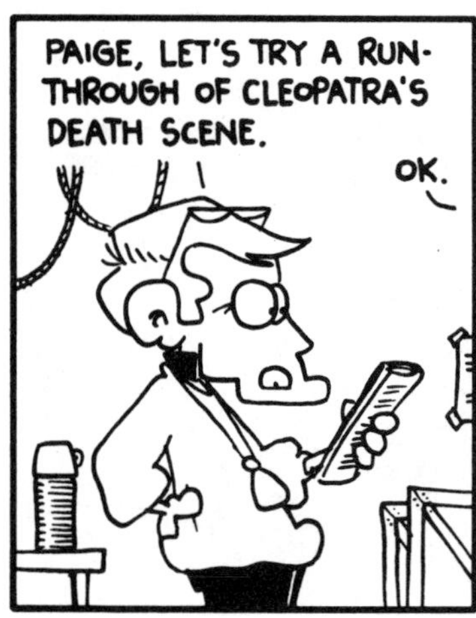
PAIGE, LET'S TRY A RUN-THROUGH OF CLEOPATRA'S DEATH SCENE.
OK.

HERE'S YOUR SNAKE.
SNAKE?! YOU WANT ME TO HOLD A SNAKE?! AAAA! GET IT AWAY FROM ME! AAAA!

GET IT AWAY!
WHAM! WHAM! WHAM!

I SAID CLEOPATRA'S DEATH, NOT THE PROP BOY'S.
HE COULD HAVE TOLD ME THE THING WAS RUBBER...
OW...
AMEND

OK, LISTEN UP, PEOPLE.

TOMORROW IS OPENING NIGHT, AND I WANT TO MAKE ONE THING PERFECTLY CLEAR...
AMEND

THINGS MAY GO WRONG. SOMEONE MAY FORGET A LINE. THAT'S THEATER. BUT REMEMBER, THE SHOW MUST GO ON! I DON'T WANT TO SEE ANY OF YOU CRYING OR PANICKING OR FALLING APART AT THE SEAMS.

...THAT'S MY JOB.
IF WE SEE SOMEONE WE KNOW IN THE AUDIENCE, IS IT OK TO WAVE?

FoxTrot
BILL AMEND

WELL, MOM, I'VE FIGURED OUT WHAT I REALLY WANT TO BE WHEN I GROW UP.
OH?

A FEDERAL AGENT IN THE X-FILES DIVISION. JUST LIKE FOX MULDER ON TV.
AMEND

THINK ABOUT IT – TRACKING DOWN UFOs, VAMPIRES, SEWER-SWIMMING LAMPREY-MEN... IT'S THE PERFECT JOB FOR SOMEONE LIKE ME – SOMEONE WILLING TO SEE FACT WHERE OTHERS SEE FICTION.

THAT CERTAINLY IS A TALENT OF YOURS.
I WONDER IF I SHOULD TRY TO REACH AGENT MULDER BY PHONE...

HELLO, FBI? I WAS WONDERING IF YOU COULD SEND ME SOME INFORMATION ABOUT BECOMING AN X-FILES AGENT.

YOU KNOW, LIKE IN THE TV SHOW. THE PEOPLE WHO INVESTIGATE THINGS LIKE UFOs AND ALIEN ENCOUNTERS AND –... HELLO? HELLO, ARE YOU THERE?

THEY KEEP HANGING UP ON ME.
AMEND

DARNED CONSPIRACY OF SILENCE.

JASON, YOU GEEK – THERE'S NO SUCH THING AS THE X-FILES! IT'S JUST A TV SHOW!
YEAH, RIGHT.

THAT'S JUST THE SORT OF THING THIS GUY SAID ABOUT THESE ANCIENT GLOW-IN-THE-DARK BUGS RIGHT BEFORE THEY CAME AND DEVOURED HIM.
AMEND

EWW.
EXACTLY. SO DON'T BE SO QUICK TO DOUBT THINGS.

SO WHERE'D YOU HEAR ABOUT THIS GUY AND THE BUGS?
ON "THE X-FILES."

I THOUGHT OF YET ANOTHER REASON WHY I'D BE A PERFECT ADDITION TO THE X-FILES TEAM.
WHICH IS?

AGENT MULDER'S FIRST NAME IS THE SAME AS MY LAST NAME. THAT MEANS THAT IF AGENT SCULLY WERE IN TROUBLE, SHE'D ONLY HAVE TO YELL "FOX" TO HAVE US BOTH COME RUNNING.

YEAH, BUT IF SHE SAYS, "FOX, YOU PINHEAD, YOU SCREWED UP AGAIN," THE WRONG FOX MIGHT TAKE OFFENSE.

NO, I WOULDN'T.
AT LEAST YOU'D BE WORKING WITH PEOPLE ACCUSTOMED TO THE UNREAL...
AMEND

I'M GOING DOWN INTO THE BASEMENT TO CHECK FOR SUPER-NATURAL ACTIVITY.
X-Files agent-in-training
AMEND

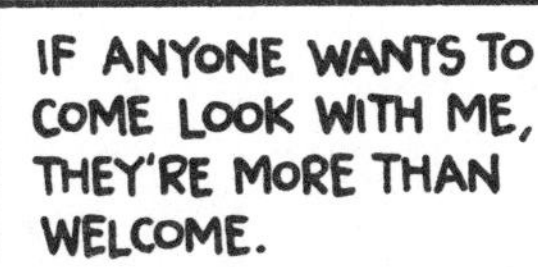
IF ANYONE WANTS TO COME LOOK WITH ME, THEY'RE MORE THAN WELCOME.

X-Files agent-in-training

PETER?... PAIGE?... ANYBODY?...
X-Files agent-in-training

WHY IS IT THAT BASEMENTS ARE ALWAYS SCARIEST WHEN YOU LEAST WANT THEM TO BE?
MORE THAN GHOSTS, I'D WORRY ABOUT PAIGE LOCKING YOU DOWN THERE.
BLAB-BER-MOUTH.

I'M NEVER GOING TO MAKE IT AS AN X-FILES AGENT AT THIS RATE.
HOW'S THAT?

I COMBED THE ENTIRE HOUSE AND COULDN'T FIND ONE LOUSY PARA-NORMAL OCCURRENCE.

NO GHOSTS... NO VAMPIRES... NO ALIEN BEINGS... NO BIGFOOTS... NO ZOMBIES... NO DISEMBODIED HEADS... NO LAMPREY-MEN COMING OUT OF THE TOILET...

SOMETIMES I HAVE THE WORST LUCK.
MIGHT I SUGGEST AN ALTERNATIVE POINT OF VIEW?
AMEND

FoxTrot

BILL AMEND

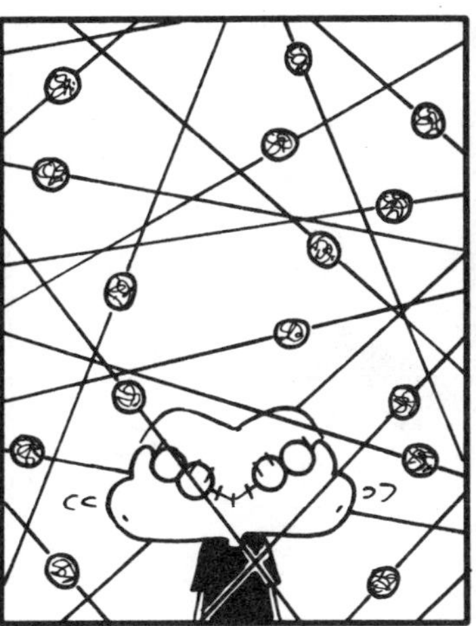

OW!
BONK!
AMEND

AND PEOPLE THINK TWO-DIMENSIONAL BILLIARDS TAKES SKILL.
I BELIEVE THIS IS YOUR SUPER BALL.

WHAT ARE YOU DOING?
WRITING MY HISTORY PAPER.

WHEN'S IT DUE?
TOMORROW.

HOW MUCH MORE DO YOU HAVE LEFT TO WRITE?
LOTS.

I NEVER SHOULD HAVE LET MYSELF GET ADDICTED TO TETRIS.
MOM, IF YOU WANT, I COULD TALK TO MARCUS ABOUT LOANING YOU HIS GAME BOY.
AMEND

WEIRDO.
NERD.

WEIRDO.
NERD.

WEIRDO.
NERD.

I BELIEVE UNDER THE RULES OF CHESS, ONE OF US MAY NOW CLAIM A DRAW.
MAKE THAT "SUPER NERD."
AMEND

BLECCH!

AAACKH!

HONGXH!

AH, THE IRONY OF HEALTH FOOD.
MEDIC...
IF PETER DIES, CAN I HAVE HIS DESSERT?
AMEND

WOW!

THAT IS INCREDIBLE!

I KNOW I WOULD!...
AMEND

ROGER, I SAID STOP WATCHING THOSE INFOMERCIALS!
DADDY, I'M ON THE PHONE.

IT WOULD APPEAR MY "DRIBBLE UMBRELLA" GAG DIDN'T GO OVER TOO WELL...
AMEND

FoxTrot

BILL AMEND

DAA... DAA... DA DA...
DA DA DA...

WHAT ARE YOU DOING?
MAKING 3-D DOT PATTERNS ENCODED WITH SUBLIMINAL MESSAGES.

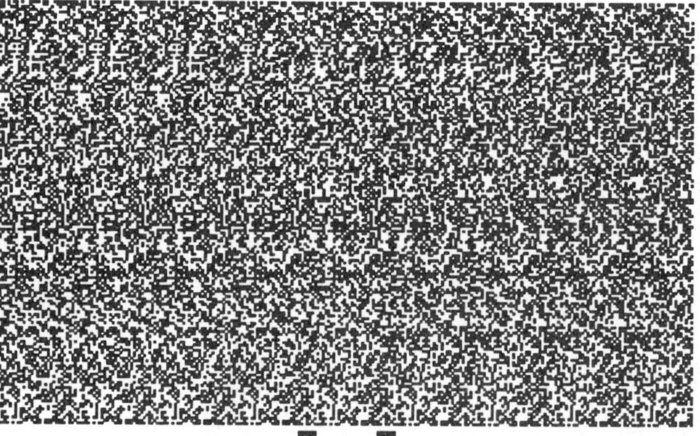
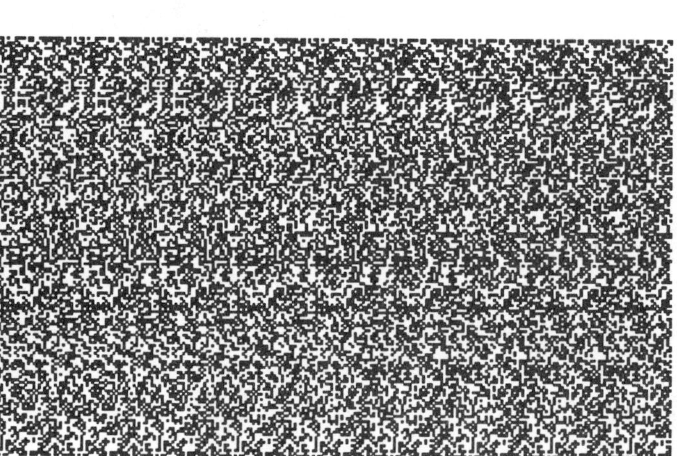

Top: BOW AND WORSHIP JASON Middle: GIVE JASON MONEY Bottom: DO JASON'S BIDDING

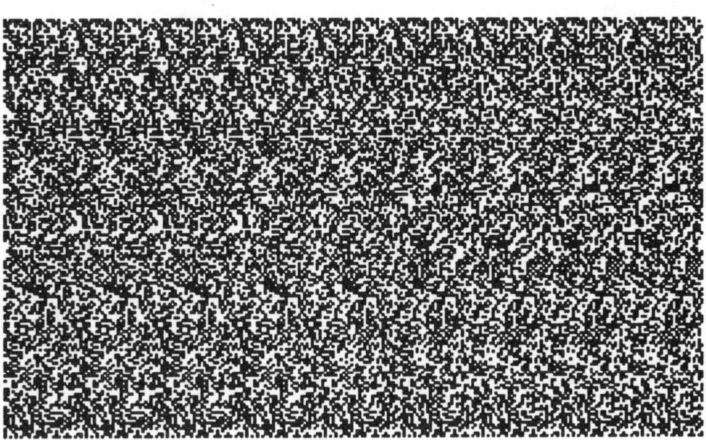

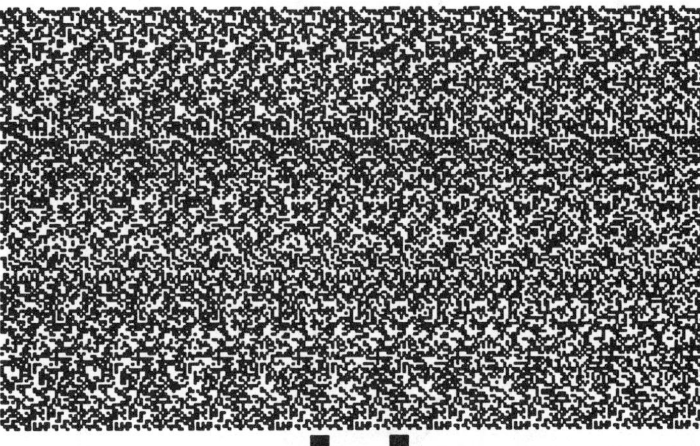

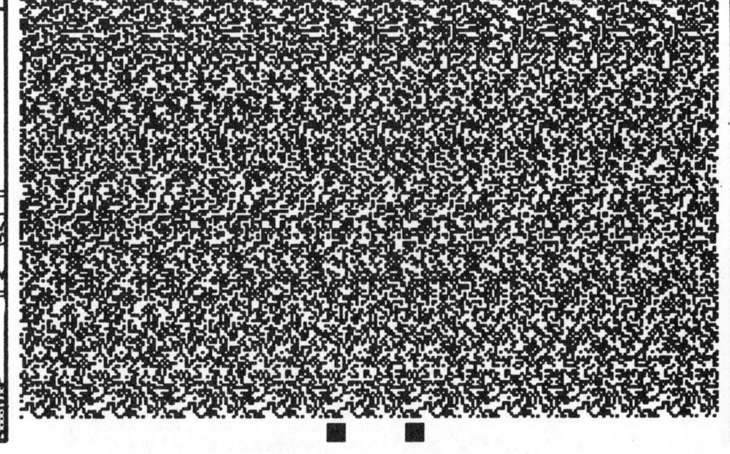

Top: BAKE JASON FOX   Middle: BUY JASON A FERRARI   Bottom: JASON IS YOUR BEST FRIEND

FoxTrot
BILL AMEND

WELCOME TO CNN'S CONTINUING COVERAGE OF THE O.J. SIMPSON TRIAL.

IN JUST A FEW MINUTES, COURT WILL RESUME AND-...

HOLD ON. THIS WAS JUST HANDED TO ME: "A SPACE-CRAFT OF SOME SORT HAS JUST TOUCHED DOWN OUTSIDE U.N. HEADQUARTERS IN NEW YORK. A SMALLISH FIGURE HAS EMERGED AND IS ADDRESSING THE CROWD."
HOLY COW.

NOW, THEN, BACK TO THE TRIAL...
I'M BEGINNING TO SEE WHY ELVIS SHOT THAT TV.
AMEND

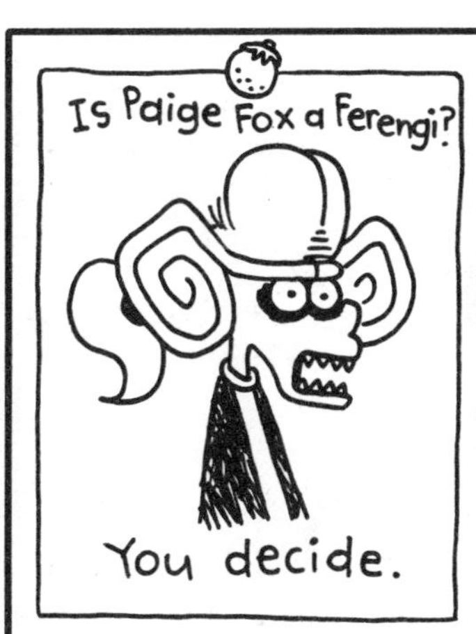
Is Paige Fox a Ferengi?
You decide.

JASON, DID YOU DO THIS?!
YES! YES! YES! YES! YES! YES! YES!
AMEND

I'VE REALLY GOT TO STOP TAKING SUCH PRIDE IN MY WORK.

WHAT ARE YOU DOING?
THIS EXTRA-CREDIT MATH PROBLEM. IT'S GOT ME TOTALLY STUMPED.

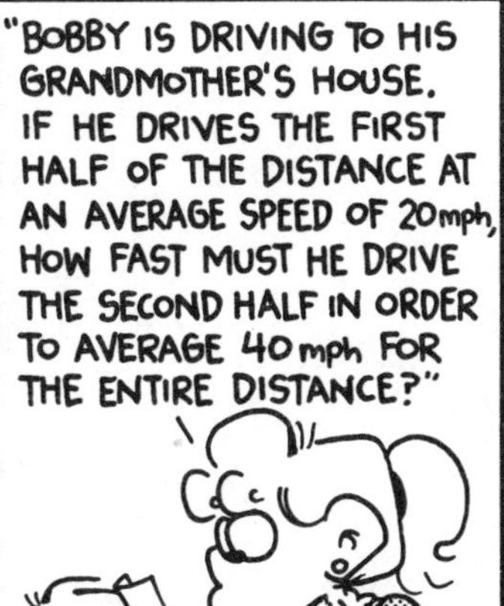
"BOBBY IS DRIVING TO HIS GRANDMOTHER'S HOUSE. IF HE DRIVES THE FIRST HALF OF THE DISTANCE AT AN AVERAGE SPEED OF 20mph, HOW FAST MUST HE DRIVE THE SECOND HALF IN ORDER TO AVERAGE 40mph FOR THE ENTIRE DISTANCE?"
AMEND

FOR $5, I'LL TELL YOU THE ANSWER.
NO WAY COULD YOU DO IT- IT'S IMPOSSIBLE!

OF ALL THE LUCKY GUESSES.
AHHH...

CHANNEL SURFING IS A LOT LIKE FIRE WALKING.
CLICK CLICK CLICK CLICK

YOU'VE GOT TO KEEP MOVING.
CLICK CLICK CLICK CLICK

...NEXT, TEEN IDOL JOEY LAWRENCE SINGS HIS-...

OTHERWISE...
CLICK CLICK CLICK CLICK
OW! OW! OW! OW! OW!
AMEND

LET'S SEE... AM I IN A BOLOGNA-AND-CHEESE-SANDWICH MOOD?...

OR A PEANUT-BUTTER-AND-JELLY-SANDWICH MOOD?...
AMEND

HMMMMM...

WHO SAYS INDECISION IS BAD?
PETER, DINNER'S IN A HALF-HOUR!

BLAH BLAH BLAH BLAH BLAH BLAH BLAH BLAH BLAH BLAH BLAH BLAH

BLAH BLAH BLAH BLAH BLAH BLAH BLAH BLAH BLAH BLAH BLAH BLAH BLAH BLAH BLAH BLAH BLAH BLAH
AMEND

BLAH-...

I HAVEN'T BEEN ON THE PHONE THAT LONG!...

FoxTrot
BILL AMEND

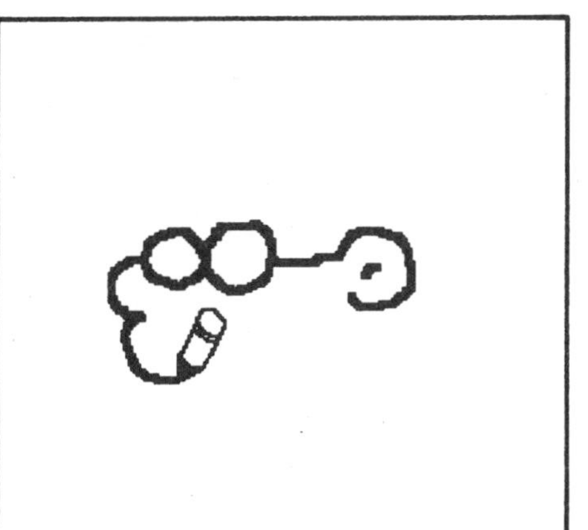

HI! I'M A GEEK!

Copy
Paste
A GEEK!

HI! I'M A GEEK!
HI! I'M A GEEK!

I'M BEGINNING TO SEE WHY YOU LIKE THIS COMPUTER SO MUCH.
TRAITOR.
AMEND

MOM, YOU LOOK AWFUL.
I KNOW.

(SNIFF) IT'S THIS DARN HAY FEVER.
AMEND

HONK!

ACTUALLY, I MEANT THAT SWEATER-SKIRT COMBINATION.
PAIGE, DON'T YOU HAVE HOMEWORK TO DO?

I CAN'T DECIDE WHAT I HATE MOST ABOUT HAY FEVER.
A

THE RUNNY NOSE... THE ITCHY EYES... THE ENDLESS SNEEZING...
PBBBTH!

AH, THE SWEET, SWEET SMELL OF SPRING!
...OR THE FACT THAT SOME PEOPLE DON'T GET IT.
WHY DON'T I GO GET YOU SOME MORE KLEENEX.
A
AMEND

WELL, TODAY I'VE CLEANED THE HOUSE...

DONE THE SHOPPING... PAID THE BILLS... REORGANIZED THE ATTIC... AND WRITTEN MOST OF NEXT YEAR'S CHRISTMAS CARDS.

AND IT'S NOT YET NOON.

THEY OUGHT TO WARN YOU ABOUT TAKING THESE ANTIHISTAMINES WITH COFFEE.
AMEND

I DING MA
HEH FEFFER ES
GEDDIG WUSS.

HUH?
I TED I DING
MA HEH FEFFER
ED GEDDIG WUDTH.

HUH??
AH DED AH
DIGG MA
HEH FEFFER
ETH GEBBIG
WODTH!

I HATE TO
SAY THIS, BUT
I THINK YOUR
HAY FEVER IS
GETTING WORSE.
I'B GOIG
BAG DO
BED.
AMEND

ROGER, YOU KNEW I HAD
ALLERGIES WHEN WE GOT
MARRIED!
UM, ANY IDEA WHERE
MY SLIPPERS WOULD BE?
AMEND

WOW. I DON'T
THINK I'VE EVER
HAD HAY FEVER
THAT BAD BEFORE.

THE SNEEZING... THE TEARY
EYES... THE CONSTANT NOSE-
BLOWING... LORD ONLY KNOWS
HOW MANY TISSUES I WENT
THROUGH THIS WEEK.

2,036.
I WAS
OFF BY
300.
HUH?

OH, WAIT—
DAD, WAS
THE POOL
SUPPOSED
TO BE
SECRET?
AM I THE
ONLY ONE
WHO VALUES
HIS OR HER TIME
AROUND HERE?!
AMEND

FoxTrot

BILL AMEND

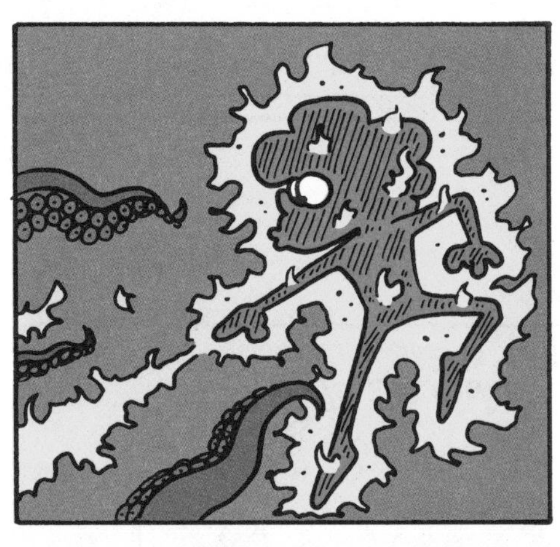

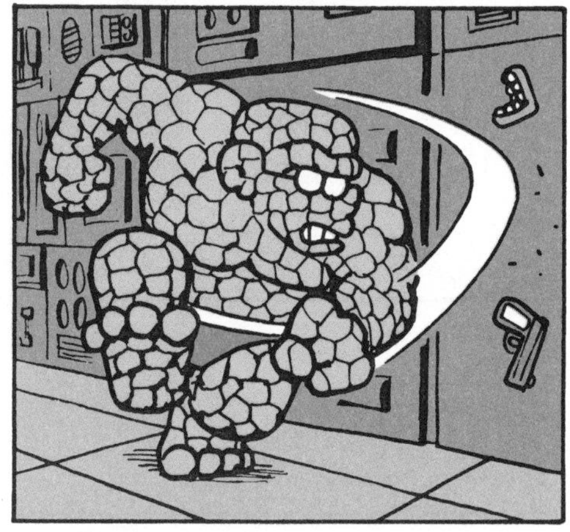

WHERE'S PETER BEEN ALL EVENING?
UP IN HIS ROOM STUDYING GENETICS.
Sports Plus

WHAT FOR?
HE'S THINKING ABOUT TAKING THE SATs NEXT MONTH.
Cartoonist to Captain Seawolf Submarine

THEY DON'T HAVE GENETICS QUESTIONS ON THE SATs.
THEN WHAT DO YOU SUPPOSE HE-
AMEND

SO IF MOM DID WELL ON VERBAL BUT DAD DID REALLY CRUMMY...
EEGAD! I'VE GOT DAD'S HAIR COLOR!
A
Genetics Made E-Z

0110100011011010010
101101001110100101101
100100011011101101011
001011101110101011010
10001100010011011100
011100101100100111011
AMEND

I THOUGHT WE AGREED, NO MORE INTERNET ON SCHOOL NIGHTS.
HEH HEH... HOW'D YOU KNOW?

...AND I THINK THAT BY CONSOLIDATING OUR-...
THUMP!

OUR...
THUMP!

CONSOLIDATING OUR-...
THUMP!
THUMP!
THUMP!
THUMP!
THUMP!
THUMP!
THUMP!
THUMP!

PEOPLE, MAYBE WE OUGHT TO CONSIDER HOLDING THESE MEETINGS **BEFORE** LUNCH.
THUMP!
ZZZZZZZ
AMEND

++++

++++

A
++++

YOU KNOW YOU'VE MADE IT RIGHT WHEN THE FUMES WAKE YOU UP.
AMEND

WHY AM I ON A DESERT ISLAND?
AMEND

WHY ARE THE COCONUT SHELLS MADE OF CHOCOLATE?

WHY IS HUNKY JIMMY ANDREWS JET-SKIING TOWARD SHORE?

NO, PAIGE, Y IS ½X².
ZZZZ... WHY DO I HEAR MY MATH TEACHER'S VOICE?
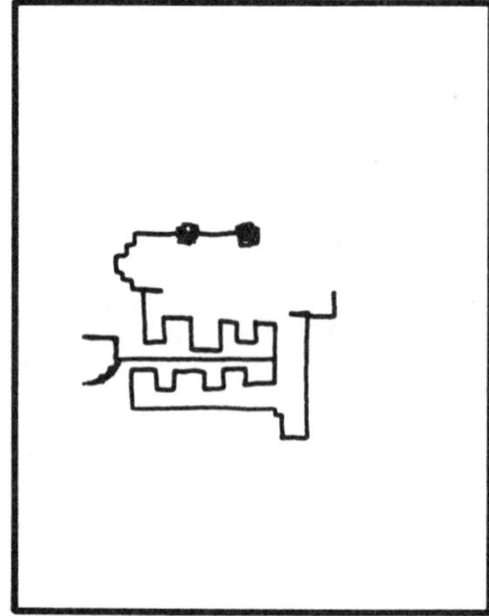
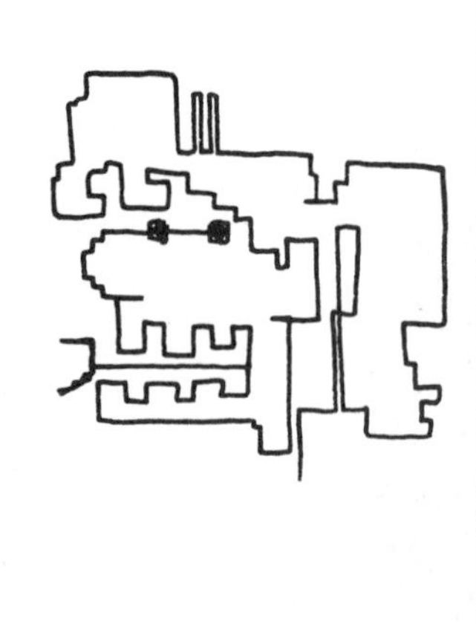

PAIGE IS A

HOW COME EVERY TIME I SEE YOU, YOU'RE SHAKING YOUR ETCH-A-SKETCH?
UM...
AMEND

FoxTrot

BILL AMEND

MOM, I'VE GOT GOOD NEWS AND BAD NEWS.
OH?

THE GOOD NEWS IS DAD'S NOT GOING TO TRY TO FIGURE OUT THE TAXES HIMSELF THIS YEAR.
JASON, THAT'S NOT JUST GOOD NEWS.

THAT'S GREAT NEWS. INCREDIBLE NEWS. THE SORT OF NEWS I'VE PRAYED TO HEAR EVERY APRIL FOR THE LAST 19 YEARS.
WHAT'S THE BAD NEWS?

HE'S DOING THEM ON THE COMPUTER.
LIKEWISE, THAT'S NOT JUST BAD NEWS...
ARE FLOPPY DISKS SUPPOSED TO SNAP IN HALF LIKE THIS?
AMEND

I DON'T GET IT – THE STUPID PROGRAM WON'T INSTALL!
DAD, DUH! YOU BOUGHT THE WINDOWS VERSION!

SO?
SO WE DON'T HAVE WINDOWS!
THE TAXINATOR
AMEND

ARE YOU NUTS?! THERE'S A WINDOW RIGHT THERE!
WOULD YOU LIKE ME TO GO NUTS?

HOW ARE THE TAXES COMING ALONG?
ANDY, PLEASE!

IT'S HARD ENOUGH TO DO THIS WITHOUT YOU LOOKING OVER MY SHOULDER EVERY TWO SECONDS!
AMEND

JUST REMEMBER THEY'RE DUE ON MONDAY.
LOOK, I KNOW WHAT I'M DOING, OK?!

...SAID GENERAL CUSTER TO HIS TROOPS.
HA-HA.
Beep Hard disk not found.

ANDY, THIS TAX SOFTWARE IS GREAT.

I JUST PUNCH IN THE NUMBERS FROM OUR W-2 FORMS AND VOILÀ, IT SAYS WE HAVE A REFUND COMING OF $37,400,591.

AMEND

NOT THAT YOU DON'T STILL NEED TO DOUBLE-CHECK ALL THE FIGURES.
REMIND ME TO BE OUT OF TOWN WHEN THE AUDIT TEAM ARRIVES.

AAAA!
WHAT HAPPENED TO MY TAX RETURNS?!
OH, IS THAT WHAT THAT BIG FILE WAS?

THE HARD DISK WAS FULL, SO I DELETED IT TO MAKE ROOM FOR MY NEW MARS COLONY SIMULATOR.
AMEND

YOU DO HAVE A BACKUP COPY SOMEWHERE, RIGHT?

DAD, DON'T THINK OF THIS AS YOUR WORST NIGHTMARE COME TRUE... THINK OF IT AS A VALUABLE LIFE LESSON.
SON, IF IT WEREN'T FOR THE FACT THAT I NEED YOU AS A DEPENDENT...
Bills
Receipts

I THINK I'VE FIGURED OUT WHY THE IRS MAKES THESE TAX FORMS SO COMPLICATED.
OH?

AFTER THE HOURS SPENT WADING THROUGH THE INSTRUCTIONS, AFTER DOING ALL THE MATH, AFTER RE-DOING ALL THE MATH, AFTER FINALLY FIGURING OUT WHAT WE OWE...

...IT'S ALMOST A RELIEF TO PUT THE CHECK IN THE MAIL.

EMPHASIS ON "ALMOST."
DO WE EVEN HAVE THIS MUCH MONEY?
AMEND

FoxTrot
BILL AMEND

FOX!...
YES, COACH?

I KNOW I USUALLY KEEP YOU ON THE BENCH. I KNOW ORDINARILY I'D MAKE YOU SIT HERE IN THE DUGOUT FOR THE WHOLE GAME.

BUT TODAY, FOX, I REALLY NEED YOUR HUSTLE.
REALLY??

HERE'S A BUCK. RUN DOWN TO THE STORE AND GET ME SOME MORE SUNFLOWER SEEDS.
YOU GOT IT, COACH!
AMEND

HERE ARE THE SUNFLOWER SEEDS YOU WANTED, COACH.
FOX, I'VE GOT BAD NEWS.

PRITCHARD'S BEEN EJECTED. I NEED YOU TO FILL IN AT SECOND WHEN WE TAKE THE FIELD.
AMEND

I'M GOING TO PLAY SECOND BASE?! I'M GOING TO PLAY SECOND BASE?!
RIGHT. NOW QUIT YAPPING AND GET READY.

BAD NEWS FOR THE OTHER TEAM IS RIGHT.
THIS DUGOUT NEEDS BEER.

FOX, I WANT YOU TO GO OUT THERE AND MAKE A DIFFERENCE.
WILL DO, COACH!

WHAP!

PETER, WHAT ARE YOU DOING?! THROW IT TO FIRST!
AMEND

I MEANT IN A GOOD WAY, FOX.
HEH HEH. SORRY.
DON'T THROW IT NOW!

IF HE BUNTS, COVER FIRST...
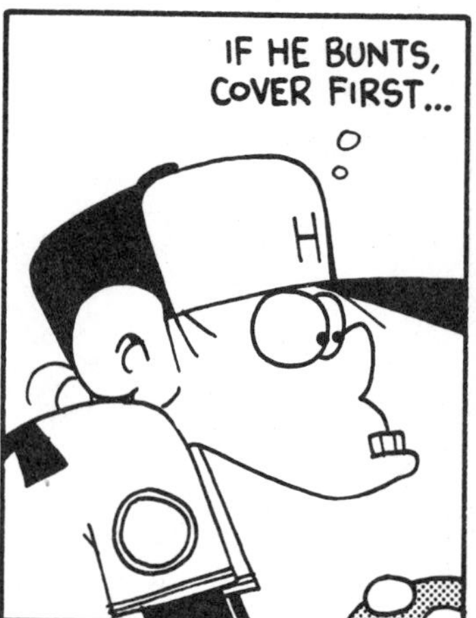
IF HE BUNTS, COVER FIRST...

IF HE —...
ZING!

IN RETROSPECT, IT PROBABLY MAKES MORE SENSE TO PLAN FOR LINE DRIVES.
NICE CATCH.
AMEND

I'VE REALLY GOT TO START TIMING MY SLIDES A LITTLE BETTER.
FOUL BALL, FOX. GO BACK TO FIRST.
AMEND

WHERE'S PETER?
HE WENT UPSTAIRS TO TAKE A SHOWER.
THYME

HOW WAS HIS BASE-BALL GAME?
LET'S PUT IT THIS WAY: THE ENTIRE TEAM MOBBED PETER, HOISTED HIM ONTO THEIR SHOULDERS AND CARRIED HIM OFF THE FIELD.

... AFTER THREE INNINGS.

OUCH. POOR KID.
THE BEST GAME I'VE BEEN TO ALL YEAR.
AMEND

FoxTrot
BILL AMEND

COWS CHEW THEIR CUD...

DOGS CHEW BONES...

KIDS CHEW GUM.
AMEND

NOT IN MY CLASS, THEY DON'T.
IS THERE A SINGLE PRIMAL INSTINCT THAT IS ALLOWED IN SCHOOL?!

ROGER, I DON'T THINK I RE-MEMBER THE LAST TIME YOU AND I WENT OUT.
SURE YOU DO.
GOLF NUT

LAST WEEKEND. WE TOOK THOSE BOTTLES DOWN TO THE RECYCLING CENTER.
AMEND

ROGER, I DON'T THINK YOU RE-MEMBER WHAT IT MEANS TO GO OUT.
WHAT ABOUT THE TRIP WE TOOK TO SEARS?

PETER, DON'T FORGET TO TAKE OUT THE TRASH.
NAG, NAG, NAG.
Sports

I HEARD THAT.
HEARD WHAT?
AMEND
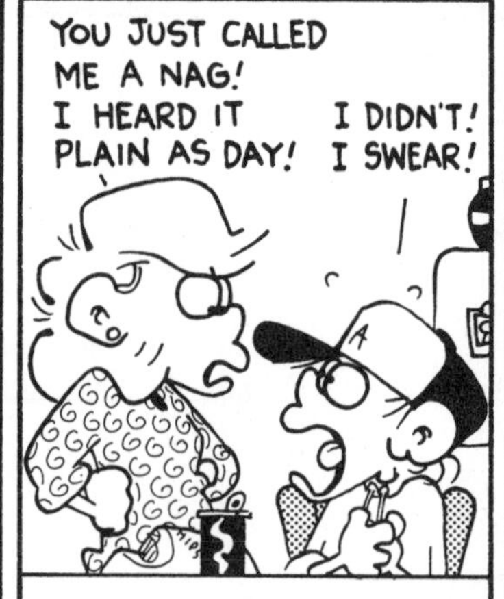
YOU JUST CALLED ME A NAG! I HEARD IT PLAIN AS DAY!
I DIDN'T! I SWEAR!

JASON, LET ME SEE THAT BOOK YOU'VE BEEN READING.
UM, WHY?

BLUE JELLO IS BY FAR MY FAVORITE.

WITH RED JELLO, YOU GET TO PRETEND IT'S GELATINIZED BRAIN JUICE, BUT WITH BLUE JELLO, IT'S MORE LIKE GELATINIZED SPACE ALIEN BRAIN JUICE.

WANNA KNOW WHAT I PRETEND THE BANANA SLICES ARE?

WHY IS IT YOU ALWAYS SEEM TO END UP WITH TWO BOWLS OF THAT STUFF?
AMEND

C'MON, FOX!

LIFT IT! LIFT IT!
AMEND

MORE! MORE! MORE!

NEVER SAY OUT LOUD THAT GYM IS YOUR EASIEST CLASS.
BETCHER VEINS DON'T DO THAT IN PHYSICS, NOW DO THEY BOY?

PAIGE, I'VE FIGURED OUT WHY YOU'RE SO AFRAID OF QUINCY.
AND WHY'S THAT?
Fox Mactor
FOURTEEN

THE TWO OF YOU NEVER HAD A CHANCE TO BOND PROPERLY.

AAAA!
AMEND

I'LL BET BY THIS TIME TOMORROW, YOU'LL BE INSEPARABLE.
JASON, IF THIS WET STUFF ON HIS CHEST IS GLUE...

FoxTrot
BILL AMEND

MOTHERRR!
PAIGE, WHAT'S WRONG?
SLAM!

THESE WEIRDOS KEEP CALLING ME UP! I DON'T EVEN KNOW WHO THEY ARE! THIS ONE GUY CALLED FROM NORWAY!

WHAT THE HECK IS GOING ON?!
WELL, IF I HAD TO GUESS...

THE INTERNET: THE ULTIMATE BATHROOM WALL.
HOW'S THIS? "FOR A REALLY, **REALLY** GOOD TIME, CALL PAIGE AT-..."

MOM, PAIGE PUNCHED ME IN THE STOMACH AND NOW I'M COUGHING UP BLOOD.

COUGH COUGH

SEE?? I THINK YOU SHOULD TAKE AWAY HER ALLOWANCE AND GIVE IT TO ME.
JASON, THAT'S KETCHUP.

YOU KNOW, IT'S POSSIBLE MY BLOOD IS JUST NATURALLY THICK AND ZESTY.
SON, JUST HOW MANY COLAS DID YOU AND MARCUS DRINK TODAY?

DR. TING, HAVE I EVER TOLD YOU WHAT A WONDERFUL TEACHER I THINK YOU ARE?

I MEAN, YOU'RE SO NICE... SO FRIENDLY... SO WITH-IT...

SO SMART...
NO, PAIGE, YOU CAN'T HAVE AN EXTENSION ON YOUR LAB REPORT.

MAYBE **TOO** SMART.
THANKS, BY THE WAY, FOR THE CHOCOLATES.
BIOLOGY

HAPPY BIRTHDAY, DENISE.
PETER, WHAT'S THIS?

IT'S ONE OF THOSE CARDS THAT LETS YOU RECORD A VOICE MESSAGE.
OOO-SOME-THING ROMANTIC AND MUSHY, I HOPE.
AMEND

ROSES ARE RED, VIOLETS ARE BLUE, MONKEYS HAVE ARM-PITS THAT SMELL BETTER THAN YOU! "X-FILES" RULES!!!
On Your Birthday

MAYBE I SHOULD GET ONE OF THESE FOR JASON'S UPCOMING FUNERAL.
GOSH, THE THINGS I MISS AS AN ONLY CHILD...

LA DEE DA...

EEEK!

WHY DOES THE HOT WATER ALWAYS SEEM TO RUN OUT WHEN I'M IN THE SHOWER?!
AMEND

SO THIS IS THE MAGIC VALVE, EH?
IS SHE OUT YET?

COMMAND POST ALPHA TO AGENT X-7, DO YOU COPY? OVER.
WHAT ARE YOU DOING?

TESTING THE RANGE OF THESE WALKIE-TALKIES WE FOUND IN AN OLD BOX IN THE BASEMENT.

MARCUS IS STARTING AT HIS HOUSE AND WALKING OVER HERE. AS SOON AS HE GETS MY SIGNAL, WE'LL KNOW EXACTLY HOW FAR AWAY THESE'LL WORK.
AMEND

COMMAND POST ALPHA TO AGENT X-7, DO YOU COPY? OVER.
WANNA KNOW WHY THEY WERE IN AN OLD BOX IN THE BASEMENT?
LOUD AND CLEAR. OVER.

FoxTrot
BILL AMEND

:SIGH: IF ONLY PETER WERE HERE...

I AM HERE, DENISE.
I MEANT ON MY SIDE OF THE SOFA.

I THINK I KNOW WHY I LIKE YOU SO MUCH, PETER.
UM, WHY, DENISE?

BECAUSE YOU'RE OBNOXIOUS.

IMMATURE. SELF-ABSORBED. THOUGHTLESS.

NOT TO MENTION REALLY, REALLY, REALLY BORING.

I MEAN, I NEVER HAVE TO WORRY ABOUT ANOTHER GIRL SNATCHING YOU AWAY!

IT'S SUCH A COMFORTABLE FEELING.
I'M GLAD YOU FEEL GOOD!

DID I MENTION "GULLIBLE"?
LET'S DISCUSS YOUR PERSONALITY FOR A SECOND...
AMEND

HERE COMES JACK PRAHL. CHECK THE LIST.
LET'S SEE...

AS OF 9:00 A.M. THIS MORNING, JACK PRAHL HAD NO PROM DATE.

YOOO HOOO... JACKIE-POOOO...

PUT A STAR NEXT TO HIS NAME – HE LOOKED OUR WAY.
WITH EXTRA-BIG EYES.
AMEND

THE PROM IS A WEEK AND A HALF AWAY AND NO ONE'S EVEN COME **CLOSE** TO ASKING ME!
PAIGE, DON'T FEEL BAD.

YOU'RE A FRESHMAN! **NOBODY** INVITES A FRESHMAN! FRESHMEN ARE DIRT! BACTERIA! HUMAN POND SCUM!

I MEAN, IF SOMEONE ACTUALLY **DID** ASK YOU, I'D BE AFRAID THEY WERE DERANGED OR SOMETHING.

PETER, AS MUCH AS I APPRECIATE YOUR ATTEMPTS TO CHEER ME UP...
HECK, **I** ONLY TALK TO YOU BECAUSE YOU'RE MY SISTER.
AMEND

YOU KNOW, PAIGE, MAYBE WE'RE GOING ABOUT THIS ALL WRONG.

MAYBE INSTEAD OF LETTING GUYS KNOW HOW DESPERATE WE ARE TO GO TO THE PROM, WE SHOULD BE PLAYING HARD TO GET.
IT'S WORTH A TRY.
AMEND

HI. I WAS, UM, WONDERING IF EITHER OF YOU WOULD CONSIDER...
IS HE TALKING TO US?
HO-HUM. I SUPPOSE SO.

(GULP) NEVER MIND.
WAIT!

The Tribune
GIRL, 14, NOT ASKED TO PROM
"Paige who?," says one boy

The Register
GIRL, 14 TO WATCH TV AT HOME WHILE REST OF SCHOOL PARTIES
Prom will be "best ever," say organizers

The Times
GIRL, 14, NAMED "MOST PATHETIC" IN NATIONWIDE POLL
"Unanimous vote," says Gallup source

I'VE GOT TO STOP NODDING OFF IN JOURNALISM CLASS.
AMEND

THIS IS RIDICULOUS, NICOLE! IT'S LIKE WE'RE THE ONLY GIRLS IN SCHOOL THAT HAVEN'T BEEN ASKED TO THE PROM!
PAIGE, THAT'S NOT TRUE.

WELL, I KNOW I'M EXAGGERATING A LITTLE, BUT...
I MEAN THE, UM, "WE" PART.

I DIDN'T KNOW HOW TO TELL YOU. BENNY WHITE ASKED ME THIS MORNING.
AMEND

EXCUSE ME WHILE I PRAY FOR THE EARTH TO SWALLOW ME UP.
THE WEIRD THING IS I THOUGHT FOR SURE HE LIKED YOU BETTER.

NICOLE, I CAN'T BELIEVE YOU SAID "YES"! I CAN'T BELIEVE YOU'RE ACTUALLY GOING TO THE PROM!

THERE YOU'LL BE, HAVING THE TIME OF YOUR LIFE WITH SOME BOY, WHILE I, YOUR BEST FRIEND SINCE FOURTH GRADE, SIT ALONE AT HOME, CRYING MY EYES OUT.

HOW CAN YOU DO THIS TO ME?!
AMEND

FoxTrot
BILL AMEND

PAIGE, WHAT DO YOU WANT ME TO DO?!

STAY HOME FROM THE PROM JUST BECAUSE YOU'RE NOT GOING?!

I CAN'T DO THAT! I'VE DREAMED OF GOING TO A PROM SINCE I WAS A LITTLE GIRL! I'VE LIVED FOR THIS OPPORTUNITY FOR AS LONG AS I CAN REMEMBER!
AMEND

LOOK, IT'LL PROBABLY BE REALLY BORING.
WHERE'S A TELEPORTATION DEVICE WHEN YOU NEED ONE?

SLAM!

PAIGE, I WISH YOU'D CALM DOWN.
CALM DOWN?! AFTER WHAT NICOLE'S DONE TO ME?!

MOTHER, SUPPOSE **YOUR** BEST FRIEND WAS GOING TO SATURDAY'S PROM WITH SOME CUTE BOY WHILE YOU WERE LEFT TO TWIDDLE YOUR THUMBS AT HOME – HOW WOULD **YOU** REACT?!

WELL, CONSIDERING THAT MY BEST FRIEND IS 45, MALE AND MARRIED...
I SWEAR, I HAVE A GOOD MIND TO STEW RIGHT THROUGH "MELROSE."
AMEND

PAIGE, SWEETIE, WHY CAN'T YOU JUST BE **HAPPY** FOR NICOLE?
WHAT??

YOU KNOW HOW MUCH THE PROM MEANS TO HER. YOU SHOULD BE HAPPY SHE'S GETTING TO GO, EVEN IF YOU AREN'T. SHE'S YOUR BEST FRIEND.
AMEND

HAPPY FOR **HER**?! SHE'S DESERTING ME, MOTHER! SHE'S LEAVING ME MISERABLE AND ALONE! SHE SHOULD BE STAYING HOME WITH **ME**!

TALK ABOUT SELFISH...
MY POINT EXACTLY!

YOU SHOULD KNOW THAT I'M NOT TALKING TO YOU ANYMORE.
WELL, I'M NOT TALKING TO **YOU** ANYMORE.

FINE.
FINE.

HEY, GUYS— WAIT UP!
AMEND

WELL, MAYBE I'LL TALK TO YOU A **LITTLE**...
MY GOD, DID YOU SEE HER SKIRT?!

NICOLE, I'M SORRY I'VE BEEN SO PETTY ABOUT THINGS.

IT'S JUST THAT I REALLY, REALLY, REALLY, **REALLY** WANTED TO GO TO THE PROM AND I'M NOT, AND WHEN I FOUND OUT YOU **WERE**, WELL, IT KINDA HIT A NERVE. WILL YOU FORGIVE ME?
YEAH.
AMEND

REALLY? JUST LIKE THAT?
REALLY.

SEE, NOW **I'D** HAVE MADE ME GROVEL.
WOULDN'T THAT BE A LITTLE, OH, WHAT'S THE WORD?

IS IT OK IF I GO TO THE MALL WITH NICOLE?
I TAKE IT THE TWO OF YOU HAVE PATCHED UP YOUR DIFFERENCES.
Atlantic

MOSTLY, YEAH. WE AGREED THAT SHE SHOULD GO TO THE PROM AND HAVE A GOOD TIME AND I SHOULD STOP WALLOWING IN SELF-PITY. LIFE'S TOO SHORT AND OUR FRIENDSHIP'S TOO IMPORTANT.
BUT THERE IS STILL A LARGER ISSUE TO RESOLVE THAT I FEAR MAY REALLY TEAR US APART.
WHICH IS?

DRESS COLOR. SHE WANTS THIS TOTALLY GROSS BLUE THING.
WELL, PAIGE, GOOD FRIENDSHIPS DO TAKE WORK.
AMEND

FoxTrot
BILL AMEND

Marry hat hey lid tell lam, ids fleas woes wide has know.

INITIATING SPELL CHECK...

BEEP. NO ERRORS FOUND.

IF YOU EVER WANT TO FEEL SUPERIOR TO A COMPUTER...
AMEND

PETER, I SPECIFICALLY ASKED YOU TO NOT FINISH THE MILK!

AND I DIDN'T! HONEST! I SWEAR!

SEE? THERE'S AT LEAST FIVE OR SIX DROPS LEFT.
YOU KNOW, IT'S KIDS LIKE YOU THAT GROW UP TO BE LAWYERS.
AMEND

If Farmer Bob's field is a circle of radius 300 meters, and A=πr²...
GEOMETRY
Paige Fox

JASON, WHAT'S PI?
3.14...

...1592653589793238462643383279502884197169399375105820974944592307816406286208 9...

MOTHER, HOW IS THIS **MY** FAULT?!
...712268066130019278766111 95909...
AMEND

HEE HEE HEE... CHECK.
THAT'S NOT A VERY SMART MOVE, ROGER.

ARE YOU KIDDING?! IT'S BRILLIANT!
ROGER, IF YOU MOVE THERE, I GUARANTEE YOU'LL BE SLEEPING ON THE SOFA EVERY NIGHT THIS WEEK.

NOW, YOU TELL ME—IS THAT SMART CHESS?

I'M BEGINNING TO SEE WHY YOU DON'T LIKE PLAYING THE COMPUTER.
HEE HEE HEE... CHECK.
AMEND

MOM, IS IT OK IF I SLEEP OVER AT MARCUS' HOUSE TONIGHT?
I SUPPOSE SO.

IS IT ALL RIGHT IF I WENT OVER THERE NOW?
I GUESS.

WOULD YOU MIND IF I SLEPT OVER TOMORROW NIGHT ALSO?
JASON, WHAT'S GOING ON?
AMEND

IT'LL BE PRETTY CLEAR IN A SECOND.
ZZZZ

HOW WAS YOUR GOLF GAME?
LET'S JUST SAY MY EVERY SHOT SEEMED TO GO IN.
AMEND

ROGER, THAT'S GREAT!
THANK YOU.
Cartoonist Captures Bigfoot

...INTO A LAKE, INTO A SAND TRAP, INTO THE PRO SHOP...
HEY, YOU DESCRIBE YOUR GAME YOUR WAY, I'LL DESCRIBE MY GAME MY WAY.

FoxTrot

BILL AMEND

AAAA! WE'RE OUT OF ALPHA-BITS!
SO?

SO I HAVE MY ENGLISH FINAL TODAY! I **ALWAYS** EAT ALPHA-BITS BEFORE AN ENGLISH TEST! THEY FUEL MY VERBAL SKILLS! WITHOUT THEM I'M DEAD!

THERE'S GOT TO BE SOMETHING I CAN DO...

LUCKY CHARMS! DO WE HAVE ANY LUCKY CHARMS?!
WOULDN'T SOMETHING **FLAKY** BE A LITTLE MORE UP YOUR ALLEY?
AMEND

STUDENTS, BEFORE I PASS OUT YOUR EXAMS, I SHOULD REMIND YOU THAT THIS TEST WILL CONSTITUTE A QUARTER OF YOUR FINAL GRADE, SO GOOD LUCK.

HERE YOU GO, MR. FOX...

HEE HEE... HEE HEE HEE... WAAA HA HA HA HA HA HA HA HA HA...

I'M SORRY. I WAS JUST STRUCK BY THE IRONY OF THE LETTER "A" ON YOUR CAP.
UM, SIR? THE CLIFFS NOTES DIDN'T MENTION THIS CHARACTER.
AMEND

WELL, STEVE, IT TOOK AN ALL-NIGHTER, BUT I DID IT.
PHYSICS

I MEMORIZED EVERY PAGE OF THIS PHYSICS TEXTBOOK. EVERY FORMULA... EVERY LAW... EVERY THEORY... COLD. TODAY'S TEST WILL BE A WALK IN THE PARK.
AMEND

SERIOUSLY, I MEMORIZED EVERYTHING.
EXCEPT MAYBE THE EXAM SCHEDULE.

AAA! TODAY'S THE HISTORY FINAL?!?...
PHYSICS IS ON FRIDAY.

I WILL NOT BE PSYCHED OUT BY MY MATH FINAL...

I WILL NOT BE PSYCHED OUT BY MY MATH FINAL...

DON'T START THE TEST UNTIL I'VE PASSED THEM ALL OUT.

I WILL NOT BE PSYCHED OUT BY MY MATH **TEACHER**, EITHER.
HEE HEE HEE...
AMEND

MISS O'MALLEY? I THINK THIS TEST HAS A MISTAKE IN IT.
OH?

QUESTION 2(a) ASKS FOR THE DECIMAL EQUIVALENT OF 1/10. THIS IS WAY TOO EASY.

SURELY YOU MEANT TO ASK FOR THE DECIMAL EQUIVALENT OF SOMETHING CHALLENGING LIKE $1/\sqrt{2}$.

I STILL DON'T UNDERSTAND WHY SHE WOULD SEND YOU HOME EARLY.
WELL, IT WAS RIGHT ABOUT THEN THAT THE PENCILS STARTED FLYING.
AMEND

IT'S SUMMER VACATION!

94 DAYS WITHOUT A SINGLE HOMEWORK ASSIGNMENT OR TEST!

94 DAYS! THAT'S 2,256 HOURS! 135,360 MINUTES! 8,121,600 SECONDS!

OF COURSE, MY MATH BRAIN WAITS UNTIL **NOW** TO SHOW UP.
AMEND

FoxTrot

BILL AMEND

JASON, I'M NOT GOING TO LET YOU SPEND THE SUMMER GLUED TO THAT TV SET.

THERE ARE A MILLION BETTER THINGS YOU COULD BE DOING WITH YOUR TIME. YOU COULD BE READING, WRITING, DRAWING... YOU COULD TAKE UP A SPORT...

HMMM. A SPORT COULD BE FUN...
IT'D BE PERFECT.

EXCUSE ME, BUT I DON'T RECALL YOU SAYING, "A SPORT **OTHER** THAN ARCHERY."
AND THE PHARMACIST WONDERS HOW I GO THROUGH ASPIRIN SO FAST.
AMEND

WHAT'S WITH THE BOW AND ARROW?
MOM WANTED ME TO TAKE UP A SPORT, SO I'M TAKING UP ARCHERY.

BULL'S-EYE!

I SEE YOU'RE ALSO TAKING UP WRESTLING.
PAIGE, LEGGO! OW!
AMEND

HEY, DAD — MOM TALKED ME INTO TAKING UP A SPORT THIS SUMMER!
JASON, THAT'S GREAT.

SO WHAT SPORT IS IT? BASEBALL? TENNIS? SOCCER? GOLF?

HERE. PUT THIS ON YOUR HEAD AND I'LL SHOW YOU.
AN APPLE?
AMEND

DAD, I'D BE A LOT MORE ACCURATE IF YOU'D STAY IN ONE PLACE.
ANNN-DYYY!...

YOU KNOW, MARCUS, IF WE GET REALLY GOOD AT THIS, MAYBE WE CAN MAKE THE '96 OLYMPIC TEAM.

TWANG!
TWANG!

WOULD THAT BE IN ARCHERY OR SPRINTING?
OF COURSE, WE'D ALSO HAVE TO BE **ALIVE** IN '96...
AMEND

I SHOT AN ARROW INTO THE AIR...

...IT FELL TO EARTH, IN PAIGE'S HAIR.

ARE YOU FAMILIAR WITH THE PHRASE "BEAT POET"?!
I SHOT ANOTHER ARROW INTO THE AIR...
AMEND

I THINK I MAY HAVE TO FIND A NEW SPORT TO PURSUE.
OH?
BUNGIE JUMPER

ARCHERY IS FUN, BUT IT'S JUST TOO DARN EXPENSIVE.
THE EQUIPMENT COSTS THAT MUCH?

WHEN YOU HAVE TO BUY IT OVER AND OVER AND OVER AGAIN.
AH...
KISS THAT BOW GOODBYE, PAL.
BUNGIE JUMPER
AMEND

FoxTrot
BILL AMEND

THAT WAY, WHEN I HAVE MY INTERVIEW AND THE DEAN OF ADMISSIONS ASKS ME WHY HE SHOULD LET ME ATTEND, I CAN RIP MY SHIRT OPEN AND SAY, "WELL, IF YOU DON'T, I'LL LOOK PRETTY STUPID FOR THE REST OF MY LIFE."

THE BEST THING ABOUT BUBBLE GUM ART IS YOU DON'T NEED NAILS TO HANG IT.
AMEND

CAN I HELP YOU?
YES. DO YOU HAVE THE SUNGLASSES THAT FOX MULDER WEARS ON "THE X-FILES"?

THAT WOULD BE THESE. I TAKE IT YOU'RE A BIG FAN OF THE SHOW.
NOT PARTICULARLY.
AMEND

THEN WHY, IF YOU DON'T MIND MY ASKING...

OH, JASONNN...
AAAA! I WANTED TO GET THOSE!

GLUG
GLUG
GLUG
GLUG
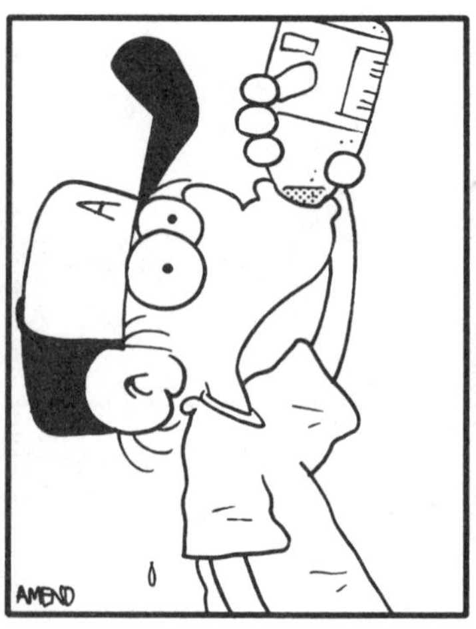
AMEND

MOM, I REALLY WISH YOU WOULDN'T STORE LEFTOVER CHICKEN BROTH IN OLD SNAPPLE BOTTLES.
I DON'T.
YOU KNOW, I THINK I WILL GO PLAY OUTSIDE...

FoxTrot
BILL AMEND

WHEN I TOLD DAD I'D MOW THE LAWN FOR FATHER'S DAY, DO YOU RECALL IF I SPECIFICALLY INDICATED THE YEAR?
FOR 80 CENTS YOU CAN GO IN HALFSIES ON THE COLOGNE SET I GOT HIM...
A
Cattleman
AMEND

A LITTLE BACON...
A LITTLE LETTUCE...
A LITTLE TOMATO...

A LITTLE LETTUCE...
A LITTLE TOMATO...
A LITTLE MORE BACON...

A LITTLE MORE TOMATO...
A LITTLE MORE BACON...
A BIT MORE LETTUCE...

A BLTLTBTBLTLB. WHY?
YOU KNOW, PETER, THERE WAS A TIME IN MY LIFE WHEN TRIPS TO THE GROCER TOOK LESS THAN FOUR HOURS.
AMEND

HI. TWO ADULTS TO SEE "DIE HARD III."
TICKETS
TICKE
SOON

YOU'D THINK THEY'D AT LEAST ASK FOR I.D. BEFORE BOUNCING US.
AMEND

I JUST LOVE THE SERVICE AT THIS PLACE.

IT'S ENOUGH TO MAKE ME WANT TO EAT LUNCH HERE EVERY DAY.
McMeals

PAIGE, THE SERVICE HERE STINKS. IT'S THE SLOWEST IN THE WORLD.
EXACTLY.

WHERE CAN PAIGE BE?! SHE'S BEEN GONE FOR TWO HOURS!
WILL YOU QUIT PACING AROUND?!
Sports Nut
AMEND

GLUG
GLUG
GLUG
GLUG
GLUG
GLUG

GLUG
GLUG
GLUG
GLUG
GLUG
GLUG

ARMED AND READY.
BOYS, HURRY UP OR WE'LL BE LATE FOR YOUR SISTER'S RECITAL!
AMEND

ANY MAIL TODAY?
JUST THE USUAL. IT'S OVER THERE.
AMEND

SOLICITATIONS FOR MONEY... SOLICITATIONS FOR MONEY... SOLICITATIONS FOR MONEY...

THIS IS GETTING RIDICULOUS.

JASON, WILL YOU STOP WRITING US THESE LETTERS?!
YOU **COULD** JUST RAISE MY ALLOWANCE.

MOM, HAVE YOU SEEN MY BACTERIA FARM ANY-WHERE?
WAS IT THAT PLATE WITH THE RED AND WHITE GUNK ALL OVER IT?
Soap Watcher

THERE WAS RED STUFF? OOO– IT'S GROWING!
I RAN IT THROUGH THE DISHWASHER. IT WAS DISGUSTING.
AMEND

YOU **WHAT**?!
YOU LEFT IT IN THE KITCHEN – WHAT DID YOU **EXPECT** ME TO DO WITH IT?!

I'D ALWAYS WONDERED WHERE MAD SCIENTISTS COME FROM.
I ALSO THREW OUT THAT DISGUST-ING BOX OF BUGS.

FoxTrot

BILL AMEND

PAIGE, DO YOU REMEMBER MARGARET O'DELL FROM MY BOOK CLUB?
THE WEIRD, PREGNANT LADY?

WELL, SHE'S NO LONGER PREGNANT. SHE WANTED TO KNOW IF YOU COULD BABY-SIT FOR HER TOMORROW NIGHT.
HOW OLD'S THE KID?

HER DAUGHTER'S NINE MONTHS. SHE ALSO WANTED TO KNOW HOW MUCH YOU CHARGE.
LET'S SEE.. NINE MONTHS IS 15 MONTHS UNDER TWO YEARS, INVERT THAT, ADD ONE AND MULTIPLY BY THE BASE RATE.

YOU KNOW, FOR SOMEONE WHO CLAIMS A "B-" IS THE BEST SHE CAN DO IN MATH...
...DIVIDE BY THE GIRL COEFFICIENT OF 1.05, ADD 50 CENTS FOR SHORT NOTICE, ROUND TO TWO DECIMAL PLACES

HI, THERE! YOU MUST BE LITTLE KATHERINE!
UM, IT'S "KATHERINE." WITH A "K."

THAT'S WHAT I SAID.
NO, YOU SAID "CATHERINE" WITH A "C." I COULD TELL.

HOLD ON — I'LL BE RIGHT BACK.

HI, THERE! YOU MUST BE THE LITTLE GIRL WHO'S GOING TO NEED MASSIVE THERAPY IN 12 YEARS!
OK, THE VIDEO CAMERA I HID IN THIS DOLL SHOULD PROVE I'M RIGHT...

OK, PAIGE, HERE ARE MY GROUND RULES...

IF THERE'S AN ACCIDENT, I WANT YOU TO CALL ME. IF SHE EATS SOMETHING SHE SHOULDN'T, I WANT YOU TO CALL ME. IF SHE CRIES FOR MORE THAN A MINUTE, I WANT YOU TO CALL ME. IF SHE SNEEZES, I WANT YOU TO CALL ME. IF SHE WETS HER DIAPER, I WANT YOU TO CALL ME. IF SHE **DOESN'T** WET HER DIAPER, I WANT YOU TO CALL ME.

THE REST ARE ON THIS LIST.

OOPS! I ALMOST FORGOT — HERE'S THE NUMBER WHERE I'LL BE.
DANG.

BYE-BYE,
SWEETHEART...

BYE-BYE,
SWEETIE-POO...

BYE-BYE,
SWEETHEART...

BY THE WAY, SHE MAY EXPERIENCE SOME SEPARATION ANXIETY.
UM, WEREN'T YOUR DINNER RESERVATIONS FOR A HALF-HOUR AGO?
AMEND

NOW, WHEN YOU CHANGE HER DIAPER, SHE LIKES IT IF YOU SING TO HER.
THIS WOMAN WON'T LEAVE.

I TOLD YOU WHICH BOTTLES TO USE, RIGHT? SHE LIKES THE PINK ONE FOR HER LATE FEEDING.
SHE WON'T LEAVE AND SHE WON'T SHUT UP.
AMEND

THERE WAS SOMETHING ELSE, TOO... NOW WHAT WAS IT?
CAN THIS BABY-SITTING JOB GET ANY MORE NIGHTMARISH?

OH, YES – I HOPE YOU DON'T MIND, BUT I DON'T OWN A TV.
DON'T SCREAM UNTIL SHE'S GONE... DON'T SCREAM UNTIL SHE'S GONE...

BYE-BYE, SWEETIE!
SAY, "BYE-BYE, MOMMY."

SAY, "HAVE FUN, MOMMY."

CLICK

WAAA!
SAY, "HURRY BACK, MOMMY."
AMEND

DON'T WORRY, KATIE – YOUR MOMMY WILL BE BACK IN A FEW HOURS.

IN THE MEANTIME, WHAT DO YOU SAY WE HAVE SOME FUN?
AMEND

OW!

KATIE, NOTICE I USED THE WORD "WE" IN THAT LAST SENTENCE.
HEE HEE GAA HEE HEE...

DON'T YOU WANT YOUR MUSHED PEAS, KATIE?

NOT EVEN A SPOONFUL?

NOT EVEN A TASTE?

YOUR MOTHER WAS RIGHT – YOU **ARE** A SMART GIRL.
PBBSPT!
AMEND

WAAA!
KATIE, YOU CAN'T BE HUNGRY **AGAIN**! I JUST FED YOU!

DO YOU WANT ME TO READ TO YOU? WHAT'S WRONG, SWEETIE?
WAAA!

SNIFF SNIFF SNIFF
AMEND

KATIE, DID YOU STEP IN DOG DOO?
WAAA!

PAG!
DID YOU JUST SAY "PAIGE"?!

PAG!
YOU DID! YOU SAID MY NAME!

KATIE, SWEETIE, YOU'RE SO CUTE! I CAN'T BELIEVE YOU SAID MY NAME! THIS IS SOMETHING I'LL NEVER FORGET!
AMEND

PAG!
...NOT THAT I WON'T **TRY** TO.

KATIE, IT'S PAST YOUR BEDTIME. LET'S GO.

COME ON, KIDDO. TIME FOR SLEEP.

LET ME EXPLAIN SOMETHING TO YOU, YOUNG LADY. BEDTIMES EXIST FOR A REASON. IF YOUR MOTHER WANTS YOU IN BED AT 9:00, YOU GO TO BED AT 9:00. NO "IFS," "ANDS" OR "BUTS." GOT IT?
AMEND

WAAAA...
ZZZZ...
AH, THE HYPOCRISY OF IT ALL...

HOW WAS BABY-SITTING?
AWFUL.

STRESSFUL. MISERABLE. EXHAUSTING.
AMEND

I TAKE IT IT PAID WELL.
HOW'D YOU KNOW?

FoxTrot
BILL AMEND

FoxTrot

BILL AMEND

FOURTEEN

FOURTEEN

QUINCY, WHAT IS THIS?!

I LEAVE YOU ALONE FOR TWO MINUTES AND YOU CHEW UP THE COVER OF PAIGE'S FAVORITE FASHION MAGAZINE?!

I EXPECT BETTER OF YOU, QUINCE, I REALLY DO!

OBVIOUSLY, I'VE FAILED TO TRAIN YOU PROPERLY.

THIS IS NOT GOOD.

I'VE TOLD YOU OVER AND OVER TO GO FOR THE **CONTENTS** FIRST!
YOU KNOW, JASON, MOST PEOPLE TRY TO **AVOID** WEARING A BODY CAST IN THE SUMMER.
A
AMEND

MOM, PETER PUT AN ICE CUBE DOWN THE BACK OF MY SHIRT!

PETER FOX, GET OVER HERE!

ARE YOU PUTTING ICE CUBES DOWN PEOPLE'S BACKS?
UM...

COULD YOU PUT ONE DOWN MINE? I'M BOILING.
MOTH-ERR!
A BIG ONE OR A LITTLE ONE?
AMEND

HEY, DAD, CHECK OUT THESE BROCHURES I PICKED UP.

THEY'RE FOR ALL THESE COOL COMPUTER CAMPS THEY'VE GOT ALL OVER THE COUNTRY. HERE'S ONE THAT STARTS NEXT WEEK.
AMEND

THINK ABOUT IT– TWO WEEKS IN THE MOUNTAINS... EATING HOT DOGS... LEARNING HOW TO USE A COMPUTER... WHAT DO YOU SAY?
SON, THEY LOOK PRETTY EXPENSIVE. DON'T YOU ALREADY KNOW HOW TO USE A COMPUTER WELL ENOUGH?

I, UM, GOT THESE FOR YOU.
OH.
DADDY, WHAT DID YOU DO TO THIS FLOPPY DISK?!

PETER, YOU'RE DRIPPING ALL OVER THE HOUSE! WHY DON'T YOU DRY YOURSELF OFF AFTER SWIMMING?!
I WASN'T SWIMMING.

THEN WHEN YOU PLAY WITH THE HOSE.
I WASN'T PLAYING WITH THE HOSE.

THEN WHEN YOU PLAY WITH WATER BALLOONS.
I WAS MOWING THE LAWN.

TAKE NOTE HOW I'LL DRY MYSELF OFF AFTER PUKING.
CALM DOWN. I'LL TAKE A SHOWER AFTER LUNCH.
AMEND

HI, HONEY.
HOW WAS
WORK?
UGGH.

VERY,
VERY,
VERY
STRESSFUL.
I'M SORRY.

AMEND

WHY DO
YOU LET
JASON
CALL ME?
RELAX—I
CONFISCATED
HIS LAUNCH
PAD.
DAD,
TALK
SOME
SENSE
INTO
MOM.

JASON, WHAT DID YOU
DO WITH ALL THOSE
EARTHWORMS YOU
DUG UP YESTERDAY?
I PUT
THEM
IN DIRT.

AND WHAT DID
YOU DO WITH
THE DIRT?
I PUT IT
IN A
CAN.
AMEND

WHAT SORT
OF CAN?
I THINK
IT WAS A
COFFEE
CAN.

MYSTERY
SOLVED,
ROGER.

WHAT'S YOUR
FORTUNE
COOKIE SAY?
"YOU ARE
ONE WHO
TAKES GREAT
CHANCES."

"...AND YOUR SISTER HAS A
MAJOR CRUSH ON SOME BOY
NAMED JIMMY HANLEY."

DID
EVERYONE
HEAR THAT?
AMEND

THAT FIRST PART
SURE WAS TRUE.
(URP)
I WISH
WE'D READ
FORTUNES
BEFORE
EATING.

FoxTrot
BILL AMEND

HI. WE'D LIKE–...
I KNOW, I KNOW, TWO TICKETS TO "APOLLO 13."
TICKETS

AND NO, WE HAVEN'T GOTTEN A NEW SHIPMENT OF THE "GENE KRANZ" COLLECTOR'S CUPS, AND YES, THERE ARE STILL SEATS AVAILABLE IN THE FRONT ROW.
AMEND

TICKETS

DO YOU GET THE SENSE THAT WE'VE DONE THIS ONCE TOO OFTEN?
THIS POP-CORN TASTES SALTIER THAN THIS MORNING'S.

MOM, CAN I SLEEP OVER AT NICOLE'S HOUSE TONIGHT?
PAIGE, YOU SLEPT OVER THERE LAST NIGHT.

...AND THE THREE NIGHTS BEFORE THAT, AS I RECALL.

WHAT'S WRONG WITH OCCASIONALLY SPENDING A NIGHT HERE AT HOME?

PRESENTING EXHIBITS A, B, C, D AND E.
WE'VE REALLY GOT TO FIND YOUR BROTHER A NEW HOBBY.
MOM, DUCK...
AMEND

WHAT DO YOU THINK OF MY NEW SUNGLASSES?
ICK.
COMICS

WHAT DO YOU THINK OF MY NEW SUNGLASSES?
SURELY YOU JEST.

WHAT DO YOU THINK OF MY NEW SUNGLASSES?
THOSE ARE THE SILLIEST LOOKING THINGS I'VE EVER SEEN.
AMEND

FINALLY, A PAIR NO ONE WILL BORROW.

AMEND

HEY, DON'T BLAME ME – BLAME BERNOULLI.

CHOC POPS

MILK
CHOC POPS
AMEND

NEXT, ON THE CBS EVENING NEWS...
I'VE REALLY GOT TO GET MY ALARM CLOCK FIXED.
WHERE HAVE YOU BEEN ALL DAY?

THERE'S ONLY ONE BIG DRAWBACK TO QUINCY'S PLASTIC IGUANA BALL.
ROLL ROLL ROLL ROLL

THYME
ROLL ROLL ROL

AAAA!
THYME

PAIGE KNOWS SOCCER.
THYME
AMEND

FoxTrot
BILL AMEND

WHAT'S WITH ALL THE MASKING TAPE?
MARCUS AND I ARE BUILDING A KITE OUT OF NEWSPAPER AND STICKS.

HERE'S THE CLASSIFIED SECTION – YOU CAN USE IT IF YOU WANT.
THAT'S OK. WE'VE GOT ABOUT 15 GROCERY BAGS FULL OF NEWSPAPERS OUT IN THE GARAGE.

OH, WHAT THE HECK- BETTER SAFE THAN SORRY.

JASON, JUST HOW BIG A KITE ARE YOU PLANNING TO MAKE?!
BY THE WAY, IF THE SUN SHOULD APPEAR TO BE BLOCKED OUT FOR LONG PERIODS THIS AFTERNOON...
AMEND

SO WHAT DO YOU THINK?
I MUST SAY I'M RELIEVED.

WHEN YOU SAID YOU WERE PLANNING TO MAKE A BIG KITE OUT OF NEWSPAPER, I FEARED YOU'D GO OVERBOARD AS YOU USUALLY DO. THIS IS A WELCOME CHANGE, JASON.

I THINK YOUR KITE IS WONDERFUL.

I DIDN'T HAVE THE HEART TO TELL HER THIS IS ONLY A 1/10-SCALE MODEL.
MAYBE WE SHOULD BUILD THE WIND TUNNEL AT MY HOUSE.
AMEND

WHAT DO YOU THINK OF OUR KITE? WE MADE IT OUT OF OLD NEWSPAPERS.
HEE HEE HEE...

HEH HEH HEH...

WAAA HA HA HA HA HA HA HA HA HA!

(SNIFF) PAIGE, COME SEE THIS!
HE MUST BE LOOKING AT THE SIDE WITH THE COMICS PAGE.
AMEND

YOU KNOW HOW IN "PEANUTS," POOR, PATHETIC CHARLIE BROWN'S KITE ALWAYS ENDS UP TANGLED IN SOME TREE?
YEAH, SO?

AT LEAST HE GETS HIS OFF THE GROUND.
GIVE US A BREAK— WE'VE ONLY BEEN AT THIS TWO HOURS!
MAYBE I SHOULD TRY RUNNING OFF THAT LEDGE OVER THERE.
AMEND

THERE'S GOT TO BE A WAY TO GET THIS KITE AIRBORNE...
WE COULD TRY RUNNING FASTER... WE COULD PRAY FOR MORE WIND... WE COULD TINKER WITH THE DESIGN...

OR...
AMEND

TOYS + MORE TOYS
DO YOU GET THE SENSE WE'RE ABOUT TO STRADDLE THE LINE BETWEEN GENIUS AND IDIOCY?
NOW, REMEMBER, WE HAVE TO TAPE THESE ON TIGHTLY.
ROCKET ENGINES
ROCKET ENGINES

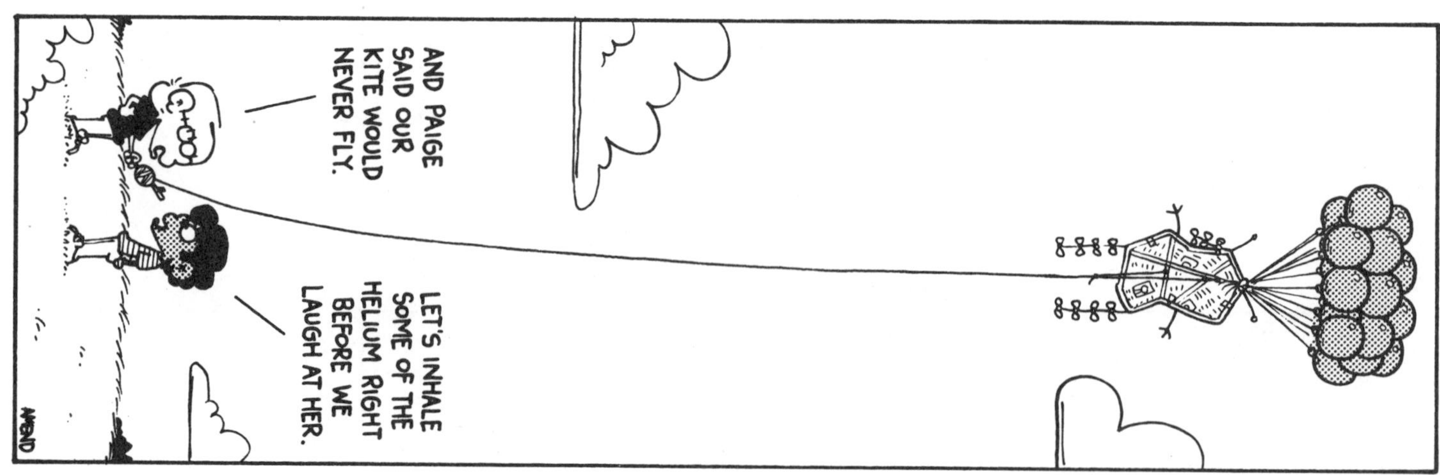
AND PAIGE SAID OUR KITE WOULD NEVER FLY.
LET'S INHALE SOME OF THE HELIUM RIGHT BEFORE WE LAUGH AT HER.
AMEND

FoxTrot
BILL AMEND

OOO – A MARS LANDER KIT FOR ONLY $19.95!
New!
Model Rockets Unlimited

OH, WAIT – IT DOESN'T ACTUALLY GO THERE.
MAYBE WE COULD SOUP IT UP...

WHY THE LONG FACES, BOYS?
WE'RE HAVING PROBLEMS WITH OUR MODEL ROCKET.

PROBLEMS WITH THE FINS?
NO.

PROBLEMS WITH THE PAINT JOB?
NO.

PROBLEMS WITH THE PARACHUTE?
NO.

WHAT, THEN?
I GUESS, MORE ACCURATELY, WE'RE HAVING PROBLEMS WITH MOM.
ROGER, HELP ME GET THE ENGINES OUT OF THIS THING.
AMEND

WANNA SEE A FOOLPROOF MAGIC TRICK?
OK.

PICK A CARD. ANY CARD.

MY PSYCHIC POWERS ARE TELLING ME SOMETHING... THEY ARE TELLING ME THAT THE CARD YOU PICKED IS... A CARD **OTHER** THAN THE FOUR OF CLUBS.
UM, THAT'S TRUE.
AMEND

TA DA! HERE– I'LL DO IT AGAIN. PICK ANOTHER CARD.
ISN'T THIS THE DECK THAT'S **MISSING** THE FOUR OF CLUBS?

WHAT ARE YOU BOYS **DOING**?!
WE FIGURED IF WE DUG A HOLE ALL THE WAY THROUGH THE EARTH'S CRUST, WE'D BE ABLE TO CREATE OUR OWN BACKYARD VOLCANO.
AMEND

BY THE WAY, DAD MIGHT WANT TO BUY SOME NEW DRILL BITS.

FIRST SHE TELLS US TO PLAY **OUTSIDE**... THEN SHE TELLS US TO PLAY **INSIDE**... THEN SHE TELLS US TO PLAY **OUTSIDE**... THEN SHE TELLS US TO PLAY **INSIDE**...
I THINK HER MISTAKE LIES IN TELLING US TO **PLAY**.

(Beep) WELCOME TO THE COMPUNET GALAXY OF ONLINE SERVICES.

UPGRADING PERIODICALS ARTWORK–PLEASE WAIT...
UPGRADING SPORTS ARTWORK–PLEASE WAIT...

UPGRADING TRAVEL ARTWORK–PLEASE WAIT...
UPGRADING MAILBOX ARTWORK–PLEASE WAIT...

HOW CONVENIENT THAT THEY CHARGE BY THE HOUR.
UPGRADING PERIODICALS ARTWORK UPGRADE–PLEASE WAIT...
AMEND

HELLO, IS THIS "LARRY KING LIVE"? AM I REALLY ON THE AIR?

YES, YOU ARE, CALLER. DO YOU HAVE A QUESTION FOR THE VICE PRESIDENT?

I CAN'T BELIEVE I GOT THROUGH! I CAN'T BELIEVE WHAT A PRIVILEGE THIS IS! A PERSON COULD WAIT HIS WHOLE LIFE FOR AN OPPORTUNITY LIKE THIS!
AMEND

CALLER, WHAT'S YOUR QUESTION?
ARE EITHER OF YOUR REFRIGERATORS RUNNING?...

AND PEOPLE THINK APOLLO 13 HAD A ROUGH FLIGHT.
UM, HOUSTON, WE HAVE ANOTHER PROBLEM...
AMEND

WANT TO BE THE FIRST TO TRY ONE OF MY BROWNIES?
NO, THANKS.

WANT TO BE THE FIRST TO TRY ONE OF MY BROWNIES?
NO, THANKS.

I GUESS THAT LEAVES ME.
AMEND

ARE YOU SURE YOU DON'T WANT TO BE THE FIRST TO TRY ONE OF MY BROWNIES?
PAIGE, I COULD SMELL THEM BAKING FOR THE LAST FIVE HOURS.

FoxTrot
BILL AMEND

Three silhouettes slowly climb a hill.

A squirrel runs for cover.

First we see a Terminator robot.

Soon he is joined by an Alien.

And a Tyrannosaurus rex.

Together they move in on their unsuspecting prey.

Cut to: Paige Fox picking flowers.

Begin musical number.

SO WHAT EXACTLY DID DISNEY SAY IN THEIR REJECTION LETTER?
YOU KNOW, MAYBE I MADE THE ENDING **TOO** HAPPY...
TWIT-HEADS, DINNER'S READY.
Jason Fox
AMEND

FoxTrot

BILL AMEND

ANDY, C'MON! THE KIDS ARE WAITING FOR US OUT IN THE CAR!
I'M NOT FINISHED PACKING!

WELL, HURRY UP! WE'RE GONNA MISS OUR FLIGHT!
I'M DOING THIS AS FAST AS I CAN!

ANDY, LET ME EXPLAIN THE SITUATION...
AMEND

IF YOU'RE NOT READY IN TWO MINUTES, THE KIDS AND I ARE GOING TO FUN-FUN UNIVERSE WITHOUT YOU.
PROM-ISE?

MY VOLUME CONTROL DOESN'T SEEM TO WORK.
YOURS IS ON **THIS** ARMREST.
AMEND

HERE ARE YOUR ROOM KEYS. THE ELEVATORS ARE JUST PAST THE SOUVENIR SHOPS.
GREAT. THANK YOU.
REGISTRATION

WILL YOU BE NEEDING A BELLHOP FOR YOUR BAGS?
THAT'S OK. I THINK WE CAN MANAGE.
REGISTRATION

OOPS, I ALMOST FORGOT—HERE ARE SOME BROCHURES HIGHLIGHTING SOME OF THE MANY WONDERFUL WAYS YOU AND YOUR FAMILY CAN SPEND MONEY WHILE HERE AT FUN-FUN UNIVERSE.

ANYTHING ELSE?
UM, ABOUT THAT BELLHOP...
REGISTRATION
AMEND

ISN'T THIS HOTEL TERRIFIC, ANDY?
MOSQUITO NEWS

HAIR DRYERS... IRONING BOARDS... A NEWSPAPER EACH MORNING... THEY'LL EVEN DELIVER A PIZZA RIGHT TO YOUR ROOM!
AMEND

IT'S JUST LIKE BEING AT HOME!
MOSQUITO NEWS

...FOR ONLY $200 A DAY.
CHECK IT OUT— FREE ICE!
MOSQUITO NEWS

MOM, THIS HOTEL IS GREAT!
I'M GLAD YOU LIKE IT.
FUN-FUN UNIVERSE

OUR ROOM CAME STOCKED WITH ALL SORTS OF CANDY BARS AND SODAS. A VERY NICE TOUCH.
REALLY? OURS DIDN'T.
AMEND

DID YOU LOOK IN THAT LITTLE REFRIGERATOR OVER THERE?
JASON, THAT'S THE MINI-BAR!

THE 20-INCH SNICKERS BARS WERE A TAD STALE, BUT OTHERWISE...
LET THE BANKRUPTCY BEGIN.
GUESS WHAT?! THE GIFT SHOPS LET YOU CHARGE THINGS TO YOUR ROOM!
FUN-FUN UNIVERSE

I'M GONNA TAKE THE UNIRAIL OVER TO THE AMUSEMENT PARK.
GIFTS
FOOD
MAP

I'M GONNA TAKE THE GLASS-BOTTOMED BOAT OVER TO THE AMUSEMENT PARK.
GIFTS
FOOD
MAP

I'M GONNA TAKE THE SKY-TUBE OVER TO THE AMUSEMENT PARK.
FOOD
GIFTS
MAP
AMEND

ISN'T IT WONDERFUL TO VACATION ALL TOGETHER AS A FAMILY?
I'M GONNA JUST STAY HERE AT THE HOTEL.

FoxTrot
BILL AMEND

I THINK WE SHOULD GO ON THE LOG RIDE NEXT.
I HATE THE LOG RIDE.

ALL THE MORE REASON...

LOOKS LIKE SOMEBODY GOT A LITTLE WET ON THE LOG RIDE.
NO KIDDING.
Fun-Fun Universe

EVERYTHING WAS GOING GREAT UNTIL WE WENT OVER THAT STUPID FINAL WATERFALL!
Fun-Fun Universe

YOU GOT NAILED BY A WAVE?
THE LID POPPED OFF JASON'S CHERRY SODA.

ICK.
THERE'S NOT A CHANCE OF RAIN TODAY, IS THERE?
THE BATHROOM WAS OUT OF PAPER TOWELS, SO I GOT YOU SOME TOILET PAPER.
Fun-Fun Universe
AMEND

AAAA! THE NEW VOODOO MOUNTAIN BOBSLED RIDE IS CLOSED FOR REPAIRS!
RELAX.

BUT IT'S SUPPOSED TO BE THE BEST ROLLER COASTER EVER!
MY FRIEND STEVE SAID THEY PRETEND TO CLOSE IT EVERY MORNING.

THAT WAY, WHEN THEY OPEN IT UP IN THE AFTERNOON AND YOU GO ON IT, YOU'LL BE SCARED TO DEATH NOT ONLY BY THE RIDE, BUT BY THE DREAD THAT THE THING WASN'T BUILT VERY WELL.
AMEND

DO YOU GET THE FEELING WE'RE IN VERY GOOD HANDS HERE?
SEE THE GUY WELDING THE TRACK? I THINK HE'S JUST A ROBOT.

HEY, PAIGE – CAN I HAVE A BITE OF YOUR COTTON CANDY?
YEAH, BUT JUST ONE.

WAD WAD WAD
WAD WAD
AMEND

AND NOW FOR MY ONE BITE...
WANT SOME SODA WITH THAT?

IT'S A FUN-FUN WORLD WHERE CHILDREN SING...

IT'S A FUN-FUN WORLD WHERE BELLS RING-A-LING...

IT'S A FUN-FUN WORLD BOTH HIGH AND LOW...
AMEND

IT'S A FUN-FUN WORLD, GO SPEND THAT DOUGH!
THAT GETS MY VOTE FOR SCARIEST RIDE.
OOO-WE'RE RIGHT NEAR SOUVENIR-LAND.
EXIT

THAT'LL BE $28.40.
FOR ONE CHILI FUN-FUN BURGER AND FRIES??
OOD FOOD FO

OOPS. MY MISTAKE.
SHEESH. I SHOULD SAY SO.
AMEND

I FORGOT THE FRIES. THAT'LL BE $41 EVEN.
OD FOOD FO

NOTHING LIKE A VACATION TO MAKE YOU APPRECIATE YOUR JOB.
ONLY ONE? PETER ATE FOUR OF THOSE.

AAAA! WHY DID I WANT TO GO ON THIS RIDE?!
CHING CHING CHING CHING

AAAA! WHAT WAS I THINKING?!
AMEND

AAAA! I MUST'VE BEEN INSANE!

IT'S NOT MY FAULT THEY MADE YOU SIT IN MY LAP.
BUTT COOTIES ARE THE WORST.
EXIT

I TELL YOU, ANDY, THERE'S NOTHING LIKE COMING HOME AFTER A LONG VACATION!

I FEEL SO ALIVE! SO ENERGIZED! SO RARIN' TO GO!

GOOD. BECAUSE ALL THESE SUITCASES NEED TO BE CARRIED UPSTAIRS.

I JUST WISH THE FEELING WEREN'T SO FLEETING.
HERE. START WITH THE HEAVIEST. THIS HAS PAIGE'S HAIR SUPPLIES.
AMEND

FoxTrot
BILL AMEND

LABOR DAY?! WHAT SADIST DECIDED TO SCHEDULE A HOLIDAY NOW?!

WE'VE HAD ALL SUMMER FOR HOLIDAYS! I DON'T WANT TO WAIT AN EXTRA DAY FOR SCHOOL TO START! I DEMAND SCHOOL NOW!
WHO'S WITH ME ON THIS?
AMEND

LA-BOR DAY?!
SWEETIE, I DON'T THINK VOLUME IS YOUR PROBLEM.

FRESH BATTERIES IN MY CALCULATOR...

FRESH PAPER IN MY BINDER...

FRESH LEAD IN MY MECHANICAL PENCIL...
AMEND

ANDY, IT'S 4 A.M.- WHAT'S GOING ON?!
CALL ME MR. BACK-TO-SCHOOL.
I'D RATHER YOU WERE MR. BACK-TO-BED.

WELCOME BACK TO SCHOOL, CLASS. I TRUST YOU ALL HAD A GOOD SUMMER VACATION.

I DON'T REALLY HAVE TOO MUCH PLANNED FOR TODAY, EXCEPT TO...UM...EXCEPT TO...
AMEND

ALL RIGHT, WHO WROTE, "GIVE REALLY HARD MATH TEST" ON MY "TO DO" LIST?!

THIS NOTE SAYS THE PRINCIPAL HAD TO RESCUE YOU FROM SOME SORT OF MOB.
IT'S BEEN THREE MONTHS! YOU'D THINK EVERYONE WOULD WANT ONE!

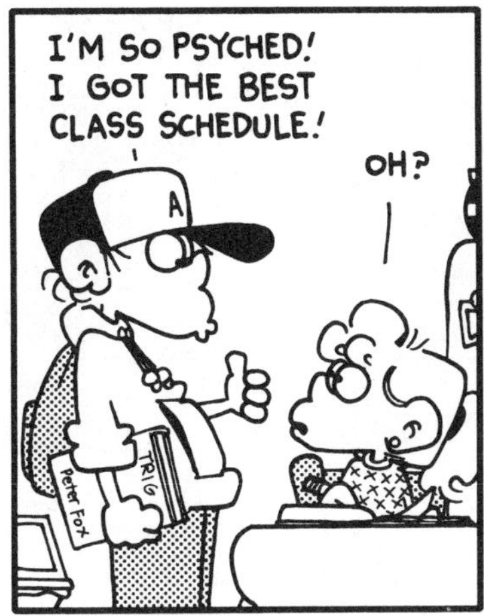
I'M SO PSYCHED! I GOT THE BEST CLASS SCHEDULE!
OH?
TRIG
Peter Fox
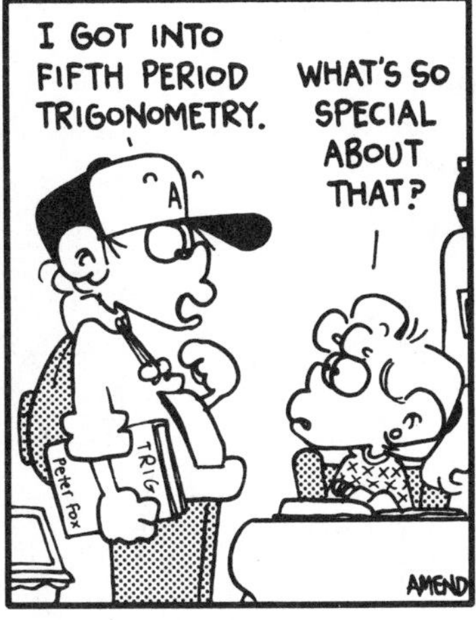
I GOT INTO FIFTH PERIOD TRIGONOMETRY.
WHAT'S SO SPECIAL ABOUT THAT?
TRIG
Peter Fox
AMEND

FIFTH PERIOD IS RIGHT AFTER LUNCH. IT'S THE PERIOD WHERE I'M MOST LIKELY TO NOD OFF.

TRIG HAS THE MOST PILLOWESQUE TEXTBOOK.
NO FAIR. IN GEOMETRY WE GOT THESE BRICK THINGS.

NICOLE, LOOK! BOBBY WHITMEYER MUST'VE TRANSFERRED INTO OUR HISTORY CLASS!

HE'S THE HUNKIEST HUNK IN THE SCHOOL! HE IS SOOO HOT! SOOO BABE-LIKE! SOOO TO DIE FOR!

...SOOO STUPID...
OH, LIKE BRAINS REALLY MATTER.
OOPS-I'M IN THE WRONG ROOM.

IN THIS CASE THEY DO.
AAAA! COME BACK!
AMEND

ROGER'S AT THE OFFICE... THE KIDS ARE BACK AT SCHOOL...
AMEND

FINALLY, I HAVE SOME PEACE AND QUIET. FINALLY, I HAVE THE HOUSE TO MYSELF.

NO MORE WAITING FOR THE KIDS TO FINISH THEIR GAMES. TODAY, I'VE GOT A CHANCE TO REALLY GET SOMETHING DONE.
BING!

LET'S SEE... NOW I'VE BEEN TO MYST ISLAND AND THE MECHANICAL AGE...
Splish Splash Clunk... Splish Splash Clunk...

FoxTrot

BILL AMEND

WHO CARES?
WHO CARES?!? PETER, IF I GET AN URGE TO PLAY "DOOMATHON," FOR EXAMPLE, I DON'T WANT TO WASTE A LOT OF PRECIOUS TIME LOOKING FOR THE DISK! I NEED IT RIGHT THAT INSTANT!

I CAN FIGURE OUT MULTI-VARIABLE CALCULUS EQUATIONS.

I CAN FIGURE OUT THE CUBE ROOT OF ANY 20-DIGIT NUMBER.

I CAN FIGURE OUT SINES AND COSINES WITHOUT CONSULTING A TABLE.
AMEND

BUT, MAN, I CAN'T FIGURE **YOU** OUT.
LOOK, I HAPPEN TO THINK "FULL HOUSE" IS FUNNY, OK?!

DADDY, YOU HAVE TO GO TALK TO JASON!
OH?
DUFFERS

HE RENTED THIS NEW "PRIMAL INSTINCT" VIDEO GAME WHERE YOU FIGHT THESE MONSTERS AND SCORE POINTS BY RIPPING THEIR HEADS OFF! YOU SEE THE VEINS DANGLING AND EVERYTHING! IT'S TOTALLY DISGUSTING AND VIOLENT!

HE'S BEEN PLAYING IT WITH MARCUS ALL EVENING!
SO YOU WANT ME TO TELL HIM HE'S TOO YOUNG FOR THIS SORT OF THING?
DUFFERS

NO, I WANT YOU TO TELL HIM TO LET ME PLAY, TOO!
WHY DO THESE SITUATIONS ALWAYS SEEM TO DEVELOP ON NIGHTS WHEN **I'M** IN CHARGE?
AMEND

JASON, YOUR STUPID IGUANA IS LOOSE AGAIN!
Verlon
Fourteen

HE'S HERE IN THE FAMILY ROOM CHEWING THROUGH THE CABLES TO YOUR NINTENDO MACHINE!

CAN'T SAY I DIDN'T TRY TO TELL YOU!
Fourteen

UM, JASON'S NOT HOME.
I KNOW.
A
Verlon
Fourteen
AMEND

FoxTrot

BILL AMEND

AAAA! I'M DEAD!
PAIGE, WHAT'S WRONG?

I HAVE TO GIVE A THREE-MINUTE SPEECH FOR MY SOCIAL STUDIES CLASS ON FRIDAY! THAT'S ONLY A FEW DAYS AWAY!

WHAT WILL I DO?! I'M DEAD! THERE'S JUST NOT ENOUGH TIME TO PREPARE!
I'M SURE YOU'LL THINK OF SOMETHING TO SAY.

SAY SCHMAY! I'LL NEED TO GET MY CUTE NEW SKIRT DRY CLEANED!
YOU KNOW, PAIGE, THE PHRASE "STYLE OVER SUBSTANCE" WASN'T MEANT TO BE A CREDO.
AMEND

NICOLE, I CAN'T BELIEVE I HAVE TO GIVE A THREE-MINUTE SPEECH FOR SOCIAL STUDIES CLASS!

MY TEACHER'S GONE INSANE! WHAT IS SHE THINKING?!

HOW CAN I POSSIBLY TALK ABOUT ANYTHING FOR THREE MINUTES STRAIGHT?!
AMEND

...SAYS THE GIRL WHO'S BEEN ON THE PHONE FOR TWO HOURS.
AND LET ME TELL YOU HOW SYMPATHETIC MY MOTHER IS BEING...

WHAT ARE YOU WATCHING?
C-SPAN.

I HAVE TO GIVE A SPEECH IN MY SOCIAL STUDIES CLASS ON FRIDAY.
Doritos

I THOUGHT WATCHING ALL THESE POLITICIANS GIVING TALKS IN NEW HAMPSHIRE MIGHT GIVE ME SOME POINTERS.
AMEND

GOING THE BROWN-NOSE ROUTE, I TAKE IT.
WELL, I DON'T HAVE TIME TO REALLY PREPARE ANYTHING TOO INSIGHTFUL.

HEH HEH HEH...
HEE HEE HEE...

WAA HA HA HA HA (COUGH) HA HA HA!
AMEND

(SNIFF) OH, MAN...

WHY THE ANGRY FACE? I THINK YOUR SPEECH'S OPENING JOKE IS REALLY FUNNY.
THERE IS NO OPENING JOKE!

OK, PAIGE, IT'S JUST A THREE-MINUTE SPEECH. DON'T BE NERVOUS.

DO WHAT DAD SAID: IMAGINE EVERYONE IS IN THEIR UNDERWEAR.

YOWZA! IT'S LIKE A CHIPPENDALES SHOW!

I'VE REALLY GOT TO STOP LISTENING TO DAD.
MISS FOX, CAN WE GET THIS STARTED SOMETIME TODAY?
AMEND

I SURVIVED MY SPEECH! I SURVIVED MY SPEECH!

I DIDN'T FAINT... I DIDN'T THROW UP... I ONLY GARBLED THREE OR FOUR WORDS...

MY SPEECH IS OVER! WEEEEEEEEE!

MISS FOX, IT'S CUSTOMARY TO DO THAT AWAY FROM THE PODIUM.
HEH HEH... SORRY.
AMEND

FoxTrot

BILL AMEND

MOM, DAD, WOULD IT BE OK FOR ME TO GET AN ADVANCE ON MY ALLOWANCE?
WHAT FOR?

DENISE AND I STARTED DATING EXACTLY ONE YEAR AGO THIS WEEK AND I WANTED TO GET HER AN ANNIVERSARY GIFT.
PETER, THAT'S SO SWEET... SO THOUGHTFUL. SO ROMANTIC.

THANKS.
OBVIOUSLY MY GENES AT WORK.
SHEESH. FORGET A WOMAN'S BIRTHDAY FOUR OR FIVE TIMES AND YOU HEAR ABOUT IT FOREVER.
AMEND

PAIGE, HELP ME OUT. I CAN'T DECIDE WHAT TO GET DENISE FOR OUR ANNIVERSARY.
LET'S SEE... YOU'VE BEEN DATING FOR ONE YEAR, RIGHT?

RIGHT.
THAT'S 52 WEEKS WITH YOU AS HER BOYFRIEND... 52 WEEKS WITH YOU AS A PIVOTAL PLAYER IN HER LIFE... 52 WEEKS WITH YOU AS THE CENTER OF HER EMOTIONAL UNIVERSE.
AMEND

ANY SUGGESTIONS?
DOES MAALOX COME GIFT-WRAPPED?

WHAT SHOULD I GET DENISE?... WHAT SHOULD I GET DENISE?...

I COULD GET HER THAT CHOCOLATE-SCENTED PERFUME. DENISE LOVES CHOCOLATE.
THERE'S NO CHOCOLATE-SCENTED PERFUME, YOU FOOL.

SURE THERE IS. THEY HAVE TV COMMERCIALS FOR IT ALL THE TIME. SHOOT – WHAT'S IT CALLED?...
AMEND

COCO. BY CHANEL.
PETER, GIVE ME THE MONEY AND LET ME GO BUY THE GIFT.

WHO AM I KIDDING? I CAN'T AFFORD TO GET DENISE ANYTHING NICE FOR OUR ANNIVERSARY.

PERFUME'S TOO EXPENSIVE... JEWELRY'S TOO EXPENSIVE... ISOTONER GLOVES ARE TOO EXPENSIVE...

YOU KNOW, SON, THERE **IS** SOMETHING EXTRA SPECIAL YOU CAN GIVE HER THAT WON'T COST YOU **ANY** MONEY.

DAD, I ALREADY TOLD YOU, I DON'T WANT YOUR OPERA TICKETS!
PLEEE-EASE??
ROGER, THOSE ARE **OURS**!
AMEND

HAPPY ANNIVERSARY, DENISE.
HAPPY ANNIVERSARY, PETER.

I, UM, WANTED TO GET YOU SOME-THING REALLY SPECIAL, BUT I COULDN'T AFFORD ANYTHING I LIKED.
THAT'S OK. TAKING THIS WALK WITH ME IS SPECIAL.

STILL, I **DO** HAVE A LITTLE GIFT FOR YOU...
WHAT ARE YOU DOING?

♪ TA DA
DID YOU TAPE WRAPPING PAPER TO YOUR **LIPS**?
AMEND

363... 364... 365.

WHAT A WONDERFUL ANNIVERSARY GIFT, PETER – A KISS FOR EVERY DAY WE'VE BEEN TOGETHER.
GLAD YOU LIKED IT.
AMEND

NOT THAT "HOURS" OR "MINUTES" WOULDN'T HAVE BEEN BETTER.
YOU KNOW, MAYBE THIS WAS A LEAP YEAR...

FoxTrot
BILL AMEND

Name: Peter Fox

Date: Not as often as I'd like to, sadly.

1. A projectile is fired from a cannon at a 30-degree angle with the ground and an initial velocity of 100 m/sec. Assuming no air resistance and g=10 m/sec², calculate the time it will spend in the air.

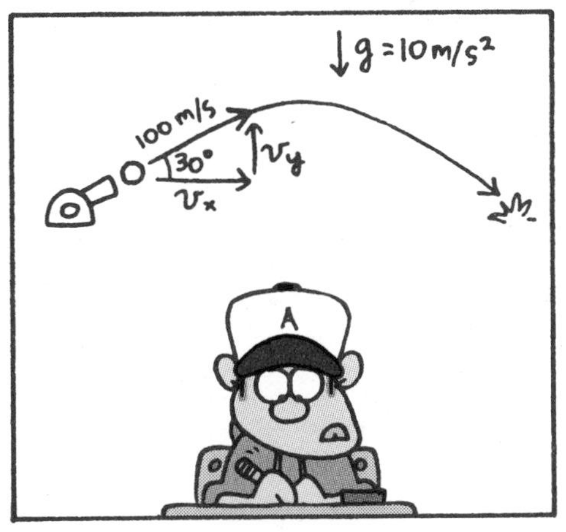
↓g=10m/s²
100 m/s
30°
v_y
v_x

Give me yar treasure! Arg! Arg!
↓g=10m/s²
Never!
100 m/s
30°
v_y
v_x
Ka-BOOM!

TIME'S UP, EVERYONE. PLEASE PASS YOUR TESTS FORWARD.

DOODLERS SHOULD NOT TAKE PHYSICS.
SHOOTING FOR AN "A" FOR "APPALLING," ARE WE, MR. FOX?
AMEND

HOW WAS SCHOOL?
GREAT! WE'RE HAVING OUR FIRST MATH TEST ON WEDNESDAY!

MISS O'MALLEY SAID IT'S GOING TO BE REALLY HARD, TOO. IT'LL COVER THE FIRST THREE CHAPTERS IN OUR TEXTBOOK.
Elementary Mathematics

SHE SAID IF PEOPLE DON'T STUDY FOR IT, THEY MAY HAVE REAL PROBLEMS GETTING A PASSING GRADE.

WELL, THEN, YOU'D BETTER GET CRACKING.
MOTHER, PLEASE. SHE WAS SPEAKING TO THE MORTALS.
AMEND

MOM SUGGESTED I STUDY SOME FOR TOMORROW'S BIG MATH TEST.

IMAGINE... **ME**, JASON FOX, KING OF MATHEMATICS, STUDYING FOR A MEASLY TEST ABOUT FRACTIONS AND DECIMALS!
Kids! Visit the Sludge Man Web Site!!!
SLUDGE MAN

HA!
AMEND

MOMS CAN BE SO FOOLISH SOMETIMES.

YOU LOOK CHIPPER.
YOU BET. TODAY'S MY MATH TEST.
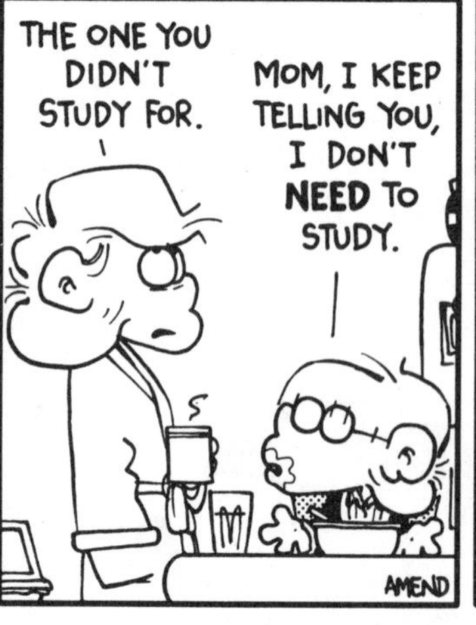
THE ONE YOU DIDN'T STUDY FOR.
MOM, I KEEP TELLING YOU, I DON'T **NEED** TO STUDY.
AMEND

WHEN IT COMES TO MATH, I'M LIKE A HUMAN SUPER-COMPUTER! THIS STUFF IS IN MY BLOOD! I CAN DO IT ALL ON INSTINCT! NO SWEAT!

...USUALLY.
JASON, I SAID TIME'S UP.

OK, EVERYONE, I'VE HAD A CHANCE TO GRADE YOUR MATH TESTS.

VERY GOOD, JASON. YOU GOT A 102. THAT'S AN A+.
AMEND

OH YESSSSSSS...

VERY, **VERY** GOOD, EILEEN. YOU GOT A 104.
OH NO!

ISN'T IT GREAT, JASON?? YOU AND I EACH GOT AN A+ ON OUR MATH TEST!

YOU GOT 102 PERCENT AND I GOT 104 PERCENT! I'VE NEVER GOTTEN AN A+ BEFORE!

I'M ACTUALLY KINDA SURPRISED YOU DIDN'T GET ALL OF THE EXTRA-CREDIT PROBLEM RIGHT. I THOUGHT IT WAS PRETTY EASY AND YOU **NORMALLY** GET THE BEST GRADE IN THE CLASS.
AMEND

YOU KNOW, FOR SOMEONE WHO JUST GOT AN A+, YOU DON'T LOOK TOO HAPPY.
WILL YOU JUST LET ME WRITHE IN PEACE?!

SWEETIE, WHAT'S WRONG?
STUPID EILEEN JACOBSON GOT A BETTER SCORE THAN ME ON THE MATH TEST!

THAT'S WHAT HAPPENS WHEN YOU DON'T STUDY.
MOTHER, THE KING OF MATH HAS BEEN DETHRONED BY A GIRL!... DID YOU HEAR ME? A **GIRL**!!!

THE LOWEST OF THE LOW! THE VILEST OF THE VILE! THE SLIMIEST OF ALL CREATURES! AND NOW ONE OF THEIR WRETCHED ILK HAS BEATEN ME AT MATH! IT'S MORE THAN I CAN STAND!

AMEND

SPEAKING AS ONE OF THE WRETCHED: "BUMMER."
I'M NOT SENSING THE KIND OF SYMPATHY I THINK I DESERVE. WHERE'S DAD?

I STILL CAN'T BELIEVE I GOT THE HIGHEST GRADE ON THE MATH TEST! IT'S LIKE A DREAM COME TRUE!

LOOK, EILEEN, THE ONLY REASON YOU GOT A HIGHER GRADE THAN ME IS BECAUSE I **LET** YOU GET A HIGHER GRADE THAN ME! OK?!

REALLY? THAT'S SO SWEET.
NO! NO! THAT'S NOT WHAT I MEANT! AAAAA!
AMEND

AAAA! AS IF IT WEREN'T BAD ENOUGH THAT EILEEN JACOBSON BEAT ME ON THE MATH TEST!...

... NOW SHE'S **LOOKING** AT ME ALL STRANGE!
HOW SO?

SAY "150-MEGAHERTZ POWERPC PROCESSOR."
150-MEGAHERTZ POWERPC PROCESSOR.

LIKE THIS.
YOU KNOW, I SHOULD THINK **MOST** PEOPLE WOULD LOOK AT YOU STRANGELY.
AMEND

WHAT DID YOU MEAN WHEN YOU SAID YOU **LET** ME GET THE HIGHEST GRADE ON THE MATH TEST?
WELL, THE TRUTH IS I DIDN'T REALLY STUDY FOR IT.

THAT'S WHY I GOOFED UP THE EXTRA-CREDIT PROBLEM. **HAD** I STUDIED, I DEFINITELY WOULD HAVE GOTTEN A PERFECT 106 PERCENT, WHICH WOULD HAVE BEATEN YOUR SCORE OF 104. INSTEAD, I GOT A LOUSY 102.
THE X FILES

LET ME GET THIS STRAIGHT: I STUDIED AND GOT MY BEST GRADE EVER; YOU **DIDN'T** STUDY AND GOT A GRADE YOU DON'T LIKE.
RIGHT. SO THAT MEANS I'M SMARTER.

UM, IF YOU SAY SO.
HECK, NAME ONE THING I STILL NEED TO LEARN!
AMEND

MY PARENTS WERE SO EXCITED THAT I GOT THE HIGH GRADE ON THE MATH TEST THAT THEY WANT TO TAKE ME OUT FOR ICE CREAM.
AMEND

I THOUGHT MAYBE YOU'D LIKE TO COME, TOO. THEY'D PAY, OF COURSE.

BOY, THAT'S A NO-BRAINER.

OH, GOOD. WE'LL PICK YOU UP AT 7:30.
WAIT! NO! YOU MISUNDERSTOOD!...

SO DO YOU WANT TO GO OUT FOR ICE CREAM WITH MY FAMILY AND ME?
WELL, I WOULD NEED MY PARENTS' PERMISSION.

AND TO BE HONEST, I REALLY DON'T SEE THEM GIVING IT TO ME.

OH.

SEEING AS I'D RATHER DIE THAN ASK.
MAYBE I SHOULD HAVE MY MOM CALL YOUR MOM...
AMEND

JASON'S GOT A DA-ATE! JASON'S GOT A DA-ATE!
IT'S NOT A DATE! HER PARENTS ARE TAKING US OUT FOR ICE CREAM!

JASON'S GOT A GIRLL-FRIEND! JASON'S GOT A GIRLL-FRIEND!
SHE'S NOT MY GIRL-FRIEND! I DON'T EVEN LIKE GIRLS!

JASON'S IN LOO-OOVE! JASON'S IN LOO-OOVE!
THIS WAS HER IDEA, NOT MINE! I'M JUST GOING FOR THE FREE CHOCOLATE SUNDAE!
AMEND

IT'S GOT TO BE TOUGH TEASING SOMEONE WHEN YOU'RE REALLY, REALLY JEALOUS.
OH, SHUT UP.

JASON, I THINK EILEEN AND HER PARENTS JUST PULLED INTO THE DRIVEWAY.

WOULD YOU MIND IF I INVITED THEM IN? WE'RE ALL SIMPLY DYING TO MEET THIS GIRL.
AMEND

OH, WAIT — THEY JUST PULLED OUT. IT MUST NOT BE THEM. NEVER MIND.

I'M NOT GOING TO ASK WHY YOU WERE WAITING FOR US OUT IN YOUR BUSHES.
ON THE WAY BACK, DO YOU THINK YOU COULD DROP ME OFF A BLOCK OR TWO AWAY?

I THINK YOU SHOULD ORDER THE KING KONG SUNDAE.
ARE YOU INSANE?! THAT'S LIKE A MILLION SCOOPS OF ICE CREAM!

C'MON, YOU'RE A GUY — YOU CAN EAT IT.
AMEND

PLEASE?? DO IT FOR ME?? PLEASE??

THIS IS NOT A GOOD SIGN, OLD BOY.
I CAN'T BELIEVE YOU REALLY ORDERED ONE OF THOSE!

LET'S SIT IN THIS LITTLE BOOTH OVER HERE.
BUT THERE'S A BIGGER BOOTH OVER THERE.

... AND ANOTHER OVER THERE.
AMEND

WHY WOULD YOU WANT TO SIT IN THE SMALLEST BOOTH THEY'VE **GOT**?!

OOPS-SORRY. IS THAT YOUR FOOT I KEEP BUMPING?
YOU NEVER ANSWERED MY QUESTION.

YOUR SUNDAE LOOKS GOOD. MIND IF I TRY SOME?
AAAA!

WHAT'S WRONG?
YOU JUST TOUCHED MY SUNDAE WITH YOUR SPOON!

SO?
THAT SPOON HAS TOUCHED YOUR LIPS! YOU'VE INFECTED MY ENTIRE KING KONG SUNDAE WITH LIP COOTIES! IT'S RUINED! IF I EAT THIS, I'LL DIE!

UM, JASON, ARE YOU IN THE FIFTH GRADE BECAUSE YOU SKIPPED A FEW YEARS?
MAYBE IF I SURGICALLY REMOVE THE REGION OF MAXIMUM CONTAMINATION...
AMEND

HEY, LOOK – THERE'S YOUR FRIEND MARCUS.
WHAT?? WHERE??

ISN'T THAT HIM OVER BY THE DOOR?
GOTTA HIDE! GOTTA HIDE!

YO, MARCUS! OVER HERE!
SPLAT!

OH, WAIT – IT'S NOT HIM.
THIS IS THE THIRD TIME TONIGHT YOU'VE DONE THIS, EILEEN.
AMEND

WELL, HOW WAS YOUR LITTLE TRIP TO THE ICE CREAM PARLOR?
UGGH. I FEEL LIKE PUKING.
THYME

COULD THAT BE FROM EATING TOO MUCH ICE CREAM?
IT'S MORE LIKELY FROM HAVING TO SIT NEXT TO GEEKY EILEEN JACOBSON ALL NIGHT.
AMEND

STILL, IT COULD JUST BE THE ICE CREAM.

FoxTrot
BILL AMEND

FoxTrot
BILL AMEND

WHAT ARE YOU DOING?
WE HAVE TO WRITE A GHOST STORY FOR ENGLISH CLASS.

MY TEACHER SAID THE SCARIER WE MAKE IT, THE BETTER THE GRADE WE'LL GET.
AMEND

SOUNDS LIKE A FUN ASSIGNMENT.
I'M CERTAINLY ENJOYING IT.

"What's to be afraid of?" thought Jason as he entered the creaky old house just before midnight...

"All I see are cobwebs," thought Jason as he surveyed the old house.

"No ghosts here," he chuckled to himself.

He was, of course, about to be proven wrong.

...BIG TIME.
SINCE WHEN DO YOU GIGGLE DOING HOMEWORK?
CHIPS
AMEND

As the clock struck 12:00, Jason had a chilling realization.

"How could that clock still be working?" he asked himself. "This house has been boarded up for 20 years!"

Suddenly, the clock became the least of his worries.

PETER, IF YOU SAW AN AX-WIELDING GHOST, WOULD YOU SAY "AAAA!" OR "AIEEE!"?
HOW COME I NEVER GET HOMEWORK ASSIGNMENTS LIKE THIS?
AMEND

As Jason ran to escape the ax-wielding ghost, the floorboards suddenly gave way.

Down, Jason fell, into the dark and murky basement.

"I wonder why the ghost didn't follow me down here," he mused.
AMEND

"Because it's already too crowded," came the reply from all directions.

"aaaa!" screamed Jason, as the ghosts raised their axes.
AMEND

Suddenly, he was at home. In his bed. It had all been just a bad dream.

Or had it?
AAAAAAA

I JUST LOVE HAPPY ENDINGS.
I THOUGHT YOU WERE WRITING A GHOST STORY.

HOW DID YOUR ENGLISH TEACHER LIKE YOUR GHOST STORY?
WELL, YOU KNOW HOW I TRIED REALLY HARD TO MAKE IT GOOD AND GORY?
Verlon
Fourteen

WHICH YOU DEFINITELY DID.
YES, WELL, I THINK I MAY HAVE DONE TOO GOOD A JOB.
AMEND
Novrel
Fourteen

HOW SO?
HE GAVE ME AN "A" PLUS...
Rovlen
Fourteen

HECK, WHAT'S WRONG WITH THAT?
I MEAN, HE GAVE ME AN "A," PLUS AN APPOINTMENT WITH THE SCHOOL COUNSELOR.
RELAX. I GET THAT ALL THE TIME.
Venrol

FoxTrot
BILL AMEND

WELL, I PROBABLY SHOULD GET STARTED ON MY BOOK REPORT.
Fax Mactor
GLAM

OH, WHAT THE HECK. THERE'S ALWAYS TOMORROW.
AMEND

ISN'T IT **DUE** TOMORROW?
YEAH, BUT THERE'S STILL TOMORROW **MORNING**.
Fax Mactor
GLAM

MY BROTHER, THE EVEL KNIEVEL OF HOMEWORK.
I GUESS I'LL NEED A BOOK. HOW LATE'S THE LIBRARY OPEN?
Fax Mactor
GLAM

MOM, WHICH WOULD BE THE BETTER WAY TO WRITE A BOOK REPORT...

TO SPEND A LITTLE TIME READING THE BOOK AND ALMOST NO TIME WRITING THE ESSAY...

OR TO SPEND A LITTLE TIME ON THE ESSAY AND ALMOST NO TIME READING THE BOOK?
HOW ABOUT PUTTING IN LOTS OF TIME ON **EACH**?

LET ME CLARIFY: A BOOK REPORT DUE IN 2½ HOURS.
"MOBY DICK"?!
AMEND

Chapter I
LOOMINGS
MOBY DICK

MOBY DICK

IF MELVILLE ONLY **KNEW**...
I HEAR YOU'VE GOT A BOOK REPORT DUE TODAY.
AMEND

WHAT ARE YOU DOING?
FLIP FLIP FLIP FLIP FLIP FLIP

I HAVE TO SOME-HOW WRITE A BOOK REPORT ON "MOBY DICK" IN THE NEXT HOUR AND A HALF BEFORE SCHOOL.
AND, OF COURSE, YOU HAVEN'T READ ANY OF IT.
AMEND
MOBY

I FIGURE MY ONLY HOPE AT THIS POINT IS TO FAN THROUGH THE PAGES AND PRAY THAT MY SUBCONSCIOUS MIND WILL ABSORB ALL THE TEXT.
I TRIED SOMETHING LIKE THAT BEFORE MY FRENCH VOCABULARY TEST.

DID IT WORK?
OUI. I MEAN, NON.

Moby Dick, by Herman Melville, is a classic American novel.

About a whale. And some sailors.

In conclusion, ...

YOU KNOW, SOME MIGHT ARGUE THAT IT'S A STROKE OF IRONIC GENIUS TO REDUCE A 432-PAGE BOOK DOWN TO SIX CHOICE SENTENCES!
PETER, YOUR NAME AND THE DATE DOESN'T COUNT AS A SENTENCE.
AMEND

DID YOU HEAR ABOUT OUR SON PETER'S LITTLE ADVENTURE THIS MORNING?

HE TRIED TO READ "MOBY DICK" AND WRITE A REPORT ABOUT IT IN THE TIME BETWEEN BREAKFAST AND SCHOOL. HIS PROCRAS-TINATION HAS GOTTEN TOTALLY OUT OF HAND.

NORMALLY, I'D WANT YOU TO GO UP AND HAVE A LITTLE TALK WITH HIM, BUT IN THIS CASE...
AMEND

... I WISH YOU'D STOP HAVING LITTLE TALKS WITH HIM!
HEE HEE... DID I EVER TELL YOU HOW I WROTE MY ENTIRE SENIOR THESIS IN ONE NIGHT?

FoxTrot
BILL AMEND

I FINALLY FIGURED OUT A WAY TO KEEP JASON FROM DIVING INTO THE LEAF PILES.
DON'T BE SO SURE...
AMEND

AARGH! THIS IS DRIVING ME NUTS!

WHY CAN'T I GET THE CHECKBOOK TO BALANCE?!

WHY?! WHY?! WHY?! WHY?! WHY?! WHY?! WHY?! WHY?! WHY?! WHY?!

...SHE ASKED RHETORICALLY.
SAY, YOU NEVER THANKED ME FOR PAYING ALL THE BILLS LAST MONTH.
AMEND

WHAT'S THE PROBLEM?
OOF!

I CAN'T GET THE LID OFF THIS PICKLE JAR.
STEP ASIDE, LITTLE BROTHER, AND LET A REAL MAN SHOW YOU HOW IT'S DONE.

NOW OBSERVE...

THIS OUGHT TO BE GOOD FOR A FEW HOURS OF LAUGHS.
HOW MUCH GLUE DID YOU USE?
OOF! OOF! OOF! OOF! Heh-Heh... OOF! OOF! OOF!...
AMEND

QUINCY, DO NOT ROLL OVER.

QUINCY, DO NOT LIE DOWN.
AMEND

QUINCY, DO NOT FETCH THE BALL.

UM, WHEN YOU TOLD ME HE OBEYED YOUR EVERY COMMAND...
QUINCY, DO NOT TAP DANCE...

...SO THEN I TOLD HIM GLOG BLURDTH UXH N INTO THE GLUFTH SOQ...

...WHICH HE TOOK TO MEAN FUB THE COMPUTER NOMF SHUMX BLOO GOOLTH!
AMEND

YOU NEVER LAUGH AT MY STORIES.
NOT THAT YOU AREN'T LAUGHABLE ON OCCASION.

THAT'S NOT DINNER YOU'RE COOKING, IS IT?
YUP. BRUSSELS SPROUT STEW.

WITH TOASTED EGGPLANT CHIPS.

AND WARM GINGER PUDDING FOR DESSERT.
AMEND

ARE YOU SURE IT'S SAFE TO SHUT OFF POWER TO THE KITCHEN?
SAFER THAN THE ALTERNATIVE.

WHICH SWEATER DO YOU LIKE BETTER, DADDY? THIS BLUE ONE...

THIS BROWN ONE...

OR THIS GREEN ONE?
I LIKE WHICHEVER ONE IS THE CHEAPEST.

YOU KNOW, APART FROM PAYING FOR ALL THIS, YOU'RE NO HELP WHATSOEVER.
THOSE ONES MARKED "90 PERCENT OFF" ARE CUTE..
AMEND

FoxTrot

BILL AMEND

FoxTrot
BILL AMEND

WHAT'S THIS?
WHAT'S WHAT?

SOMEONE PUT A NOTE IN MY LOCKER.
IT WASN'T ME. WHAT'S IT SAY?

YOWZA.
A NOTE THAT SAYS "YOWZA"? HOW VERY, VERY ODD.
AMEND

I CAN'T BELIEVE SOMEONE REALLY LEFT ME THIS NOTE!
LET ME SEE! LET ME SEE!

Dear Paige,
I think you are totally cute.
Love,
Your secret admirer

THINGS LIKE THIS NEVER HAPPEN TO ME!
APPARENTLY, THAT'S CHANGED.
AMEND

UM, THIS **IS** MY LOCKER, RIGHT?
AND YOUR NAME **IS** PAIGE...

I'VE GOT A SECRET ADMIIIRER...

I'VE GOT A SECRET ADMIIIRER...
SAT. 7:30 PM

NCE
T.
0 PM

YOU'VE GOT TO LOOK WHERE YOU'RE WALLLKING...
I'VE (OUCH) GOT A SECRET ADMIIIRER...
AMEND

LOOK, NICOLE! HE WROTE ME ANOTHER NOTE!
NO WAY! WHAT'S IT SAY?!

Dear Paige,
I think you are the hottest girl in the entire school.
Love,
Your secret admirer
AMEND

OBVIOUSLY, I DON'T KNOW ANYTHING ABOUT THIS GUY...

...BUT I CAN TELL HE IS **VERY** PERCEPTIVE.
NONSENSE. HE'S OBVIOUSLY SOMEHOW OVERLOOKED **ME**.

MOM, DID YOU EVER GET NOTES FROM A SECRET ADMIRER WHEN YOU WERE IN SCHOOL?
NOT IN SCHOOL, BUT THE YEAR AFTER COLLEGE I DID.

I WAS LIVING IN AN APARTMENT AND SOME-ONE KEPT SLIPPING ANONYMOUS LOVE LETTERS UNDER MY DOOR.

DID YOU EVER MEET HIM?! WHAT WAS HE LIKE?!
WELL, HE TURNED OUT TO BE A REAL NERD. NOT AT ALL WHAT I EXPECTED.
AMEND

OH.
...BUT I MARRIED HIM ANYWAY.
I HEARD THAT.

THIS SECRET ADMIRER OF MINE MUST REALLY, REALLY LIKE ME.

HIS FIRST NOTE SAID I WAS TOTALLY CUTE, HIS NEXT ONE SAID I WAS TOTALLY HOT AND TODAY'S NOTE SAYS I'M TOTALLY PERFECT.

I WONDER WHAT HIS **NEXT** NOTE WILL SAY...
AMEND

HOW ABOUT "TOTALLY GODDESS-LIKE"?
I CAN'T BELIEVE MY STUPID SISTER IS FALLING FOR THESE.

IT'S 3:45. MY SECRET ADMIRER'S NOTE SAID HE'D MEET ME HERE AT 2:30.

AMEND

I'LL GIVE HIM ANOTHER HOUR AND THAT'S IT.

WHY, HELLO PAIGE...
PETER, GO AWAY! I'M EXPECTING SOMEONE!

A SECRET ADMIRER, PERCHANCE?
HOW DID YOU-...?
AMEND

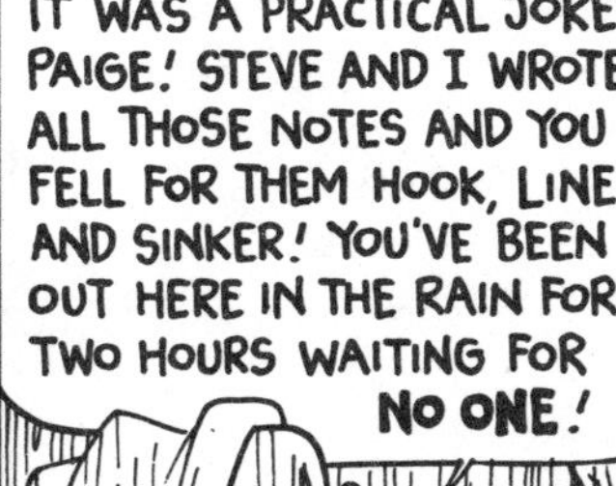
IT WAS A PRACTICAL JOKE, PAIGE! STEVE AND I WROTE ALL THOSE NOTES AND YOU FELL FOR THEM HOOK, LINE AND SINKER! YOU'VE BEEN OUT HERE IN THE RAIN FOR TWO HOURS WAITING FOR NO ONE!

WELL, IF YOU'RE NOT GOING TO LAUGH, I WILL.
SOME-HOW, I IMAGINED HELL WOULD BE WARMER THAN THIS.

PAIGE, C'MON – IT WAS A JOKE!
AMEND

A GAG!

IT WAS FUNNY!

HONESTLY, SOME PEOPLE JUST HAVE NO SENSE OF HUMOR.
YOU'RE TELLING ME.

PAIGE, SWEETIE, I KNOW YOU'RE HURTING.

I KNOW YOU'D PROBABLY LIKE NOTHING BETTER RIGHT NOW THAN TO PUNCH YOUR BROTHER PETER'S LIGHTS OUT.

BUT IF YOU COULD JUST PUT ASIDE THAT ANGER FOR A SECOND...
AMEND

PAIGE? UM, I'M REALLY, REALLY SORRY.
PETER, IS THAT CATCHER'S MASK REALLY NECESSARY?
I CAN'T HEAR YOU, PETER. STEP A LITTLE CLOSER...

PAIGE, GEEZ– I SAID I WAS **SORRY**.
PETER, WHAT YOU DID TO ME TODAY WAS AS MEAN AS ANYTHING YOU'VE EVER DONE.
Fourteen

THIS PAST WEEK, WHEN I READ THOSE NOTES, FOR THE FIRST TIME IN MY LIFE I FELT REALLY ATTRACTIVE AND SPECIAL. I FELT LIKE SOMEONE OUT THERE REALLY CARED ABOUT ME. AND TODAY WAS THE DAY I WAS GOING TO MEET HIM. DO YOU HAVE ANY IDEA HOW HAPPY AND NERVOUS AND EXCITED I WAS?!

THEN **YOU** POP OUT AND LAUGH, "HA HA HA, SUCKER– IT WAS ALL JUST A JOKE!" WELL, IT WASN'T A JOKE TO ME AND IT CERTAINLY WASN'T WHAT I WOULD CALL **FUNNY**!
AMEND

BUT HOW WAS **I** SUPPOSED TO KNOW THAT?
PETER, YOU **ARE** SORRY.

PAIGE IS PRETTY MAD AT YOU, HUH?
YEAH.

I PULLED A PRETTY THOUGHTLESS PRANK ON HER AT SCHOOL. I DIDN'T REALIZE SHE WOULD TAKE IT SO HARD.

SHE SAYS THERE'S NOTHING I CAN DO TO MAKE UP FOR WHAT I DID.

UM, SINCE WHEN DO **YOU** BAKE COOKIES?
SHE DID SAY THERE ARE WAYS I CAN **BEGIN** TO MAKE UP...
AMEND

FoxTrot
BILL AMEND

WHO WANTS TO GO CHRISTMAS SHOPPING WITH ME? PETER??
PAIGE, GET A LIFE! IT'S NOT EVEN DECEMBER!

SO WHAT? **TELL** ME YOU'RE NOT DYING TO HIT THE MALLS! **TELL** ME YOU DON'T LIE AWAKE AT NIGHT PLANNING WHAT STORES YOU'LL GO TO FIRST! **TELL** ME YOU DON'T CHOKE ON YOUR DROOL EVERY TIME YOU HEAR THE WORD "NORDSTROM"!

DON'T LIE—I CAN SEE IT IN YOUR EYES.

OH, WAIT-THAT'S MY REFLECTION.
PAIGE, I'M GOING TO COUNT TO 10, AS QUICKLY AS I CAN...
AMEND

HOW'S YOUR NEW VIDEO GAME?
GREAT, I THINK. I HAVEN'T REALLY PLAYED IT YET.

THEN WHAT ARE YOU DOING?
THESE GAMES ALWAYS HAVE SECRET CHEAT CODES THAT MAKE YOU INVINCIBLE AND STUFF, SO I'M METHODICALLY TRYING EVERY BUTTON COMBINATION, HOPING TO FIND ONE. ONCE I DO, I CAN GO ON THE INTERNET AND TRADE FOR ALL THE REST.
AMEND

I SHOULD BE READY TO PLAY THIS NEXT TUESDAY OR WEDNESDAY.

I SEE A LOT OF BOARD GAMES COMING YOUR WAY THIS CHRISTMAS.
I MEAN, WHAT'S THE POINT OF PLAYING IF YOU CAN'T WIN EVERY TIME?

"...NEVER SEND TO KNOW FOR WHOM THE BELCH TOLLS; IT TOLLS FOR THEE."
"**BELL**," YOU MORON.
FOURTEEN

IT'S "FOR WHOM THE **BELL** TOLLS"!
FOURTEEN
AMEND

BRAAAP!

I BELIEVE YOU STAND CORRECTED.
YOU KNOW, MY FRIENDS AT SCHOOL THINK I MAKE THESE STORIES UP.

Mary Beth has baked
an apple pie.
Math

Her father wants a piece twice as big as her mother's piece. Her brother wants a piece twice as big as Mary Beth's piece. Mary Beth wants a piece 2/3 as big as her father's piece.
Math

If she divides the pie so that no extra pieces remain, what fraction of the pie goes to her brother?
Math

First of all, why she would even give any pie to her brother...
BAD NEWS, PAIGE. QUINCY THREW UP ON YOUR TOOTHBRUSH.
AMEND

THIS WORLD WIDE WEB IS PRETTY COOL. I MEAN, IF I WANTED TO, I COULD ACCESS NASA PHOTOS...

I COULD GO INTO THE LIBRARY OF CONGRESS AND READ HISTORICAL TEXTS...

I COULD STUDY THE ART COLLECTIONS OF NUMEROUS EUROPEAN MUSEUMS...

EMPHASIS ON "IF YOU WANTED TO."
OOO-MISS DECEMBER LIKES ICE CREAM! ME, TOO!
AMEND

NUCLEAR MISSILES CAN'T DESTROY PLASMA-MAN.

LASERS ONLY MAKE HIM STRONGER.

HE'S IMPERVIOUS TO EVERY WEAPON TECHNOLOGY KNOWN TO MAN.

BUT SPILL ONE LOUSY GLASS OF GRAPE JUICE...
HERE'S A SPONGE. IS IT RUINED?
AMEND

FoxTrot
BILL AMEND

FoxTrot
BILL AMEND

NEIMAN MARCUS?! YOU WENT SHOP-PING AT NEIMAN MARCUS?!
HUH?
Neiman Marcus

ISN'T THEIR STUFF GREAT?! ISN'T THEIR STUFF AMAZING?! WHADJA GET?! LEMME SEE! LEMME SEE!
Neiman Marcus

Neiman Marcus
AMEND

TWO QUESTIONS: DID YOU GET THAT DEAD RAT OUT OF THE BASEMENT, AND WHAT ON **EARTH** HAS GOTTEN INTO YOUR SISTER?!
MOM, NEXT TIME I ASK FOR A PAPER BAG...
THYME

HEY, JASON – UP FOR A GAME OF CHESS?
SURE. CAN I BE WHITE?
CHESS PIECES

OK.
E2 - E4
F1 - C4
D1 - F3
F3 × F7
CHECKMATE. I WIN.
AMEND

THANKS, DAD, THAT WAS FUN.
CHESS PIECES

METHINKS MY GAME MAY BE GETTING A BIT TOO PREDICTABLE.
CHESS PIECES

PAIGE, YOUR MOTHER ASKED ME TO MAKE YOU KIDS' LUNCHES TODAY. WHAT KIND OF SANDWICH DO YOU LIKE?

OH, I DON'T CARE. PEANUT BUTTER AND JELLY... BOLOGNA AND CHEESE... TUNA FISH... WHATEVER.

GOTCHA.

MY FATHER IS NOT OF THIS EARTH.
A PEANUT BUTTER, TUNA FISH, BOLOGNA, JELLY AND CHEESE SANDWICH?!
AMEND

PETER, I'M DOING A PROJECT FOR SCHOOL.
OK...

WOULD YOU SAY THIS GLASS IS HALF-FULL OR HALF-EMPTY?
IS THAT ROOT BEER?

UM, YEAH.

EMPTY.
THAT **WASN'T** ONE OF THE CHOICES!
AMEND

HMM. UNLESS MY FURNITURE IS SHRINKING ALONG **WITH** ME...
I THINK MOM GOT OUR LAUNDRY MIXED UP.
AMEND

I JUST LOVE EGGNOG. IT'S SO RICH...
Freakos

SO CREAMY...

SO FESTIVE...
Freakos

SO OPAQUE...
OPAQUENESS IS KEY.
JASON, IF YOU HIDE **ONE MORE** FAKE SPIDER IN MY GLASS...
Freakos
AMEND

FoxTrot
BILL AMEND

FLOUR

SCROOOOOGE...
SCROOOOOGE...
JASON, I TOLD YOU, I'M NOT RAISING YOUR ALLOWANCE AND THAT'S **FINAL**!
AMEND

FoxTrot
BILL AMEND

A BLANKET OF SNOW OUTDOORS...

A CRACKLING FIRE IN THE FIREPLACE...

A BIG MUG OF HOT COCOA...
JOHNNY MATHIS ON THE STEREO...
Peter
Paige

YOU KNOW, ROGER, THIS REALLY MAY BE ONE OF OUR NICEST CHRISTMAS EVES EVER.

THEY WERE OUT OF "IT'S A WONDERFUL LIFE," SO WE RENTED "TERMINATOR 2."
...WIDE-SCREEN EDITION.
GIVEN OUR TRACK RECORD, THAT MAY NOT BE TOO DIFFICULT.
SPEAKING OF WHICH, I'D BETTER CHECK ON PAIGE'S COOKIES.
I COULDN'T FIND THE BAKING SODA, SO I USED DIET PEPSI. IS THAT OK?
AMEND

AAAA! DOOMATHON II! I GOT DOOMATHON II!

IT'S SUPPOSED TO BE THE BEST COMPUTER GAME EVER! EXPLODING BULLETS... SLO-MO DECAPITATIONS... 16-BIT STEREO GUT-SPLATTER SOUND EFFECTS... OVER 10 TIMES THE KILLING ACTION OF DOOMATHON I...
AMEND

OH, THANK YOU, SANTA! THANK YOU! THANK YOU!

I MUST'VE BEEN EXTRA NICE THIS YEAR.

JASON, I DON'T LIKE YOU PLAYING THIS COMPUTER GAME. IT'S TOO VIOLENT.
BUT SANTA GAVE IT TO ME!
San Fran

SANTA MADE A MISTAKE.
BUT LOOK AT HOW MUCH **FUN** IT IS!...

Blam! Blam! Blam! Blam! Blam! Blam! Blam!
San Fran
AMEND

GOSH, ALL THE THRILLS OF A BUTCHER SHOP.
WAIT–IT'LL GET BETTER ONCE I FIND THE BAZOOKA.

I'M TELLING YOU, MOM, YOU'LL CHANGE YOUR OPINION OF DOOMATHON II ONCE YOU'VE PLAYED IT.
JASON, I REALLY DON'T THINK SO.

LOOK OUT! THERE'S A CYBER-GHOUL! SHOOT HIM!
Blam! Blam! Blam! Blam! Blam! Blam! Blam! Blam! Splat!

WAY TO GO, MOM! YOU BLEW HIS HEAD OFF!
I DON'T MIND TELLING YOU, JASON, THIS IS VERY, VERY DISTURBING.
AMEND

BECAUSE IT'S SO GORY?
BECAUSE I WANT TO KEEP PLAYING. OOO– I FOUND A BIGGER SHOTGUN.

MOM, CAN I USE THE COM-PUTER AT SOME POINT? IT IS, AFTER ALL, MY GAME.
JUST LET ME PLAY A FEW MORE MINUTES...

Blam! Blam! Blam! Blam! Blam! Blam! Blam! Blam! Blam! Blam! Blam!

Blam! Blam! Blam! Blam! Blam! Blam! Blam! Blam! Blam! Blam! Blam!

MOM, C'MON, THAT'S WHAT YOU SAID LAST NIGHT.
YOU MISSED A GREAT SUNRISE, BY THE WAY.
AMEND

ANDY, LOOK AT YOU! YOU'VE BEEN PLAYING THAT DOOMATHON GAME ALL WEEK!

YOU DON'T EAT... YOU DON'T SLEEP... FOR YEARS YOU'VE RAILED AGAINST VIOLENCE IN VIDEO GAMES AND HERE YOU ARE, GLUED TO THE WORST OF THE LOT!
AMEND

WHAT DO YOU HAVE TO SAY FOR YOURSELF?!
I NEED MORE COFFEE— MY TRIGGER FINGER IS SLOWING DOWN.

YOU KNOW, YOU WEREN'T THIS SYMPATHETIC WHEN I WENT ON MY TWISTER BINGE.

WHERE HAVE YOU BEEN?

AT THE COM-PUTER STORE. I TRADED IN MY DOOMATHON II GAME FOR SIM-MOONWALK.
HOW COME?
AMEND

MOM CONVINCED ME THAT I WAS TOO YOUNG TO HAVE A GAME LIKE THAT IN THE HOUSE.
BUT I THOUGHT SHE LIKED IT— SHE'S BEEN PLAYING IT NIGHT AND DAY.

THAT'S WHAT CONVINCED ME. I MEAN, I CAN'T DO MY LAUNDRY.
I GUESS THIS MEANS NO MORE FROOT LOOPS FOR DINNER.
NOW I'LL NEVER KNOW THE SECRET TO LEVEL 83!

FoxTrot
BILL AMEND

WHAT'S WITH **YOU**?
THIS NEW YEAR IS OFF TO ONE MISERABLE START.

SOMEONE ATE ALL THE CHOCO HONEY FLAKES, I SQUIRTED MY EYE WITH THIS STUPID GRAPEFRUIT, AND TO TOP IT ALL OFF, THERE'S NO "CALVIN" IN THE COMICS!

LOOK ON THE BRIGHT SIDE, PAIGE — THINGS COULD BE WAY WORSE.
OH, YEAH? HOW?

HEH HEH, HAVE YOU BEEN IN YOUR CLOSET LATELY?
JASON, IF THAT IGUANA CHEWED UP ANY MORE OF MY SHOES...
AMEND

MOM, I'M AFRAID TO ASK, BUT WHAT'S FOR DINNER?
I THOUGHT I'D MAKE A PIZZA.

PIZZA?! **FINALLY** SOMETHING **NORMAL**! FINALLY SOMETHING OTHER THAN YOUR TOFU CASSEROLE OR THAT WHEAT GERM STEW OR THOSE NOXIOUS BEET AND EGGPLANT BROWNIES! FINALLY! FINALLY! FINALLY!

AND I'M REALLY HUNGRY, TOO.

UM, WHAT'S WITH THE CARTON OF LIMA BEANS?
YOU DIDN'T ASK WHAT **SORT** OF PIZZA...
AMEND

WHAT ARE YOU DOING?
I'M WRITING A COMPUTER VIRUS THAT I'M GOING TO STICK ON THE INTERNET.

IT'S DESIGNED TO INFECT THE MACHINES OF USERS OF THE alt.government.-conspiracy.-paranoid NEWSGROUP.

AT A RANDOM DATE, THEIR SCREENS WILL GO BLACK, SPUTTER FOR A SECOND, THEN DISPLAY THE MESSAGE, "THEY ARE COMING."

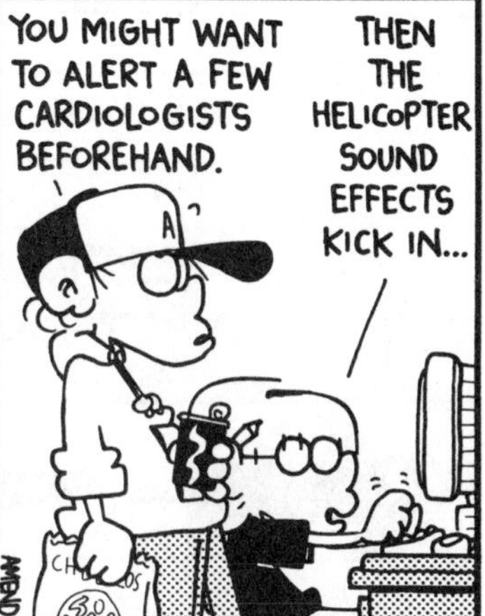

YOU MIGHT WANT TO ALERT A FEW CARDIOLOGISTS BEFOREHAND.
THEN THE HELICOPTER SOUND EFFECTS KICK IN...

AAAA! WE'RE OUT OF COFFEE?! WE CAN'T BE! NOT TODAY!

I'VE GOT TO GIVE A PRESENTATION IN TWO HOURS! WE'RE OUT OF INSTANT, TOO?! AAAA!
I GOT THE LAST CUP, DAD. SORRY.

AMEND

LET'S SEE... I'LL HAVE FOUR DOUBLE HULKBURGERS.
SINCE WHEN DID YOU TURN INTO MISTER MONEYBAGS?

I AM UNIQUE!

I AM SPECIAL!

I HAVE WORTH!
AMEND

SO HOW COME ALL I SEE IS THAT ZIT ON MY CHIN?

AAAA! WHO RECORDED OVER MY "X-FILES" TAPE?! I GOT UP EXTRA EARLY JUST TO SEE IT! I'VE BEEN WAITING ALL WEEK FOR THIS!

SOMEONE IN THIS FAMILY IS A BONE-HEADED VCR MORON AND I INTEND TO FIND OUT WHO! HEADS WILL ROLL!
AMEND

OH, WAIT – THIS ISN'T MY "X-FILES" TAPE. MINE MUST BE THIS OTHER ONE.

FALSE ALARM, PEOPLE – GO BACK TO SLEEP.
ONE YOUNG HEAD IS ABOUT TO ROLL...

FoxTrot
BILL AMEND

AH, HERE'S THE ONE I WAS LOOKING FOR.

JASON, NOBODY BUILDS A SNOW-MAN ONE FLAKE AT A TIME!
KEEP YOUR EYES PEELED FOR AN EQUILATERAL DODECAGON.

HEY, PAIGE, IT SNOWED LIKE 18 INCHES!
I KNOW. SO?
Toridos

I THOUGHT MAYBE YOU'D WANT TO GO OUT AND MAKE ONE OF YOUR TRADEMARK PAIGE FOX SNOWMEN.
JASON, I'M WATCHING TV.

PLEASE? JUST ONE?
I SAID I'M BUSY.

PAIGE, PLEASE?? NO ONE ELSE CAN MAKE THEM QUITE THE WAY YOU DO. THEY'RE JUST SO PER-FECTLY CUTE!
JASON, NO!

GREAT.

WELL, WE'VE GOT TO FEED HIM SOMETHING.
I'M THINKING... I'M THINKING...
AMEND

WELCOME TO COMPUNET!

YOU'VE GOT MAIL!
REALLY?! YEEHA!

Jason –
Just a reminder that you promised to clean your room before dinner.
– Love, Mom
AMEND

IT REALLY **IS** GETTING DANGEROUS FOR KIDS TO GO ONLINE.
YOU'LL NOTICE **I** HAVEN'T LOGGED ON IN TWO MONTHS.
SPORTS NUT DIGEST

I CAN'T BELIEVE HOW TRASHY THIS TALK SHOW IS.

IT'S NOTHING BUT SEX, VULGARITY, DEVIANCY AND FIGHTING. IT HAS NOT ONE REDEEMING VALUE. NO THOUGHTFUL DISCUSSIONS... NO GOOD EXAMPLES... NOTHING BUT PURE, 100 PERCENT TRASH.
AMEND

SO WHY DO YOU WATCH IT?
I JUST TOLD YOU.

ANY IDEA WHY MOM IS OUTSIDE SCREAMING?
HOOT! HOOT! HOOT!

OK, EVERYONE, I'VE FINISHED GRADING YOUR TESTS.

MR. FOX...

A "99"?! I GOT A "99"?! I KNEW IT! I KNEW IT! I'M GONNA **OWN** THIS SEMESTER!
YOU'RE HOLDING IT UPSIDE-DOWN.

OH. HEH-HEH.
PEOPLE, THIS MIGHT BE A GOOD TIME TO DISCUSS THE CURVE...
AMEND

MOM! PAIGE IS TAKING THE LAST HO-HO!
IT'S MINE! I HAD DIBS!
HO-HOS

MOM SAID I COULD HAVE IT IF I DID MY HOMEWORK, SO GIVE IT UP!
DIBS HAVE PRECEDENCE! ASK ANYBODY! LET GO!

LET'S SEE... WHAT WAS IT SOLOMON SUGGESTED UNDER THESE CIRCUMSTANCES?
AMEND

SOMETHING ABOUT CUTTING KIDS IN HALF?
NO, NO, I INSIST...
HERE, PAIGE, YOU TAKE IT.
HO-HOS

I'M JUST A HUNKA-HUNKA BURNIN' LOVE... WOOOO...

I'M JUST A HUNKA-HUNKA BURNIN' LOVE... OH, YEAH...

I'M JUST A HUNKA-HUNKA BURNIN' LOVE... YESSIR...

HUNKA-HUNKA-HUNKA BURNIN'-BURNIN'-BURNIN'...
JASON, DOWN IN THE BASEMENT, THERE'S A VALVE MARKED "COLD WATER SHUTOFF"...
I THOUGHT YOU'D NEVER ASK.
AMEND

HEY, PAIGE, CHECK IT OUT— I MADE A SNOWMAN THAT LOOKS JUST LIKE YOU!

AND SO CONVENIENTLY IN THE MIDDLE OF THE STREET.
OH, LOOK— HERE COMES A PLOW...
AMEND

PETER, I THOUGHT WE AGREED, NO "DONKEY KONG" UNTIL YOUR HOMEWORK IS DONE.
MOM, MOM, MOM.

YOU MISUNDERSTOOD. WHAT I SAID WAS, NO HOMEWORK UNTIL "DONKEY KONG" IS DONE.

AND WHEN WILL **THAT** BE?
BEST I CAN FIGURE, MID- TO LATE APRIL.
AMEND

CARE TO EXPLAIN THESE SHARDS OF PLASTIC IN THE CARPET?
YOU KNOW HOW, ON OCCASION, MOM HAS NO SENSE OF HUMOR?
PHYSICS

I TELL YOU, NICOLE, WHEN THE CAFETERIA HAS PIZZA FOR LUNCH, IT'S LIKE ALL MY TROUBLES DISAPPEAR.

I MEAN, WHO **CARES** ABOUT A DUMB SHAKESPEARE QUIZ?! WHO **CARES** THAT I'VE GOT A LAB REPORT DUE?! WHO **CARES** THAT I LEFT MY BOOK BAG AT HOME?! I'M GOING TO HAVE **PIZZA**! WELL, I'D BETTER GO GET IN LINE.
AMEND

DON'T YOU KEEP YOUR WALLET IN YOUR BOOK BAG?

YOU CAN HAVE MY YOGURT...
THE IRONY GODS MUST BE ROLLING ON THE FLOOR.

WHAT ARE YOU DOING?
AIMING MY SPEAKERS INTO THE FLOOR.

THIS WAY, I CAN LISTEN TO MY STEREO WHILE I'M DOWNSTAIRS DOING MY HOMEWORK IN THE DINING ROOM, WHICH HAPPENS TO BE RIGHT BENEATH US. NOW ALL I HAVE TO DO IS CRANK UP THE VOLUME.

WHAT'S THAT NOISE?
THAT'S THE MUSIC. IT'S KINDA MUTED FROM THE CARPETING.

NO, IT SOUNDED MORE LIKE A CHANDELIER CRASHING.
SAY, WERE THE PICTURES ON MY WALL ALWAYS THIS CROOKED?
AMEND

WHAT'S ALL THIS?
JUST A LITTLE AFTERNOON SNACK.

GRAPES? PEARS? RADISHES? AN ASSORTMENT OF DRIED FRUITS?

OH, SWEETIE, I'M SO PROUD!
AMEND

MOM'S ACTING AWFULLY WEIRD TODAY, QUINCE.

I WON!

I WON! I CAN'T BELIEVE I **WON**!
AMEND

THE PROBLEM WITH PLAYING SOLITAIRE IS YOU NEVER GET TO **GLOAT**.

BATTER UP!

PAFF!

YOU KNOW, SNOW **TENNIS** MIGHT BE FUN, TOO.
OOF– THIS ONE I'LL PITCH UNDERHAND...
AMEND

FoxTrot
BILL AMEND

ROGER... KIDS... WANNA DRIVE OVER TO THAT NEW BOOKSTORE?

PERHAPS YOU DIDN'T HEAR ME...

THERE'S NOTHING LIKE GOING INTO A BIG BOOKSTORE ON A COLD WINTER EVENING...
LOCAL AUTHORS

FINDING A COLLECTION OF SHORT STORIES THAT YOU'D ALWAYS MEANT TO READ...

TAKING OFF YOUR COAT...
PLOPPING DOWN IN THEIR CAFÉ...

AND WATCHING SHOPPERS COME AND GO AS YOU SIT BACK AND SIP ON COFFEE.

AH, BLISS.

AH, REALITY.
MOM, DID YOU BRING YOUR CREDIT CARD? THEY HAVE EVERY "STAR TREK" BOOK.
SINCE CALENDARS ARE HALF-PRICE, CAN I GET NIKI AND STEPHANIE?
FOURTH AND ONE AND THEY'RE PUNTING?!
AT LEAST THIS PLACE SELLS T-SHIRTS.
Read Me, Seymour!
AMEND

PETER, YOU DRANK THIS WHOLE POT OF COFFEE?!
I NEED THE CAFFEINE FOR THIS MORNING'S MATH TEST.

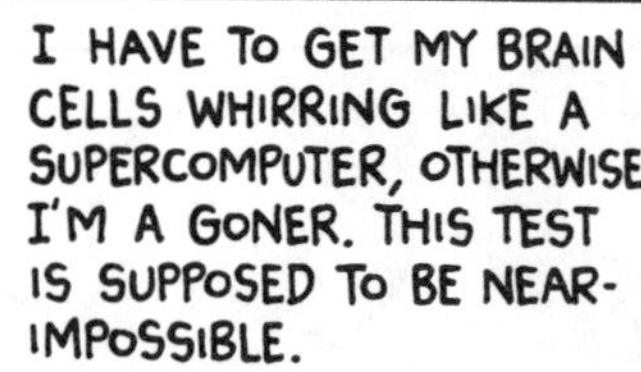
I HAVE TO GET MY BRAIN CELLS WHIRRING LIKE A SUPERCOMPUTER, OTHERWISE I'M A GONER. THIS TEST IS SUPPOSED TO BE NEAR-IMPOSSIBLE.

I FIGURE AFTER EIGHT CUPS I'M BOUND TO BE ONE LIGHTNING-FAST COMPUTATION MACHINE.

IF THE BOYS' BATHROOM IS 150 FEET AWAY AND I RUN AT A RATE OF 20 FEET PER SECOND...
MR. FOX, IS THERE A REASON YOU KEEP SQUIRMING?
AMEND

THEY CANCELED SCHOOL BECAUSE OF THE SNOW!

THEY CANCELED SCHOOL! THEY CANCELED SCHOOL!
AMEND

THEY-...

JUST WHO DO THEY THINK THEY ARE?!
NICE TRY.

HEE HEE HEE...
WHAT ARE YOU DOING?

MISTING MY SNOWBALLS WITH WATER SO THEY'LL TURN INTO ICEBALLS. I'M DECLARING ALL-OUT WAR ON PAIGE.
HERE SHE COMES NOW.
AMEND

HEY, PAIGE, YOU MANGY SEWER SPORE- I HOPE YOU'RE PRE-PARED FOR A PUMMELING!

HAVE FUN.
UH-OH.
OH, I AM READY, BELIEVE ME...

HI. I'D LIKE A SLICE OF PIZZA WITH PEPPERONI...
Today's Special

...MUSHROOMS... SAUSAGE... BLACK OLIVES... ONIONS... ARTICHOKE HEARTS... PEPPERONI...
YOU ALREADY SAID PEPPER-ONI.

I KNOW. I MEAN ANOTHER LAYER OF IT.
Today's Special

...ANCHOVIES... SAUSAGE... EXTRA CHEESE...
LUIGI, YOUR FAVORITE CUSTOMER IS BACK.
TELL HIM I'M STILL CLEANING THE OVEN FROM HIS LAST VISIT!
Tomorrow's Special
AMEND

POTATO CHIPS... PRETZELS... HOT DOG BUNS...
WHAT ARE YOU DOING?

MAKING MY PRE-SUPER BOWL CHECKLIST.
AMEND

I LIKE TO MAKE SURE I'VE GOT ALL THE SUPPLIES I'LL NEED AHEAD OF TIME. THAT WAY, I CAN AVOID A MAD DASH TO THE STORE ON SUNDAY. I RECOMMEND THIS FOR ANYONE.

ASPIRIN... ANTACID... EAR PLUGS...
HAVE YOU SEEN MY LUCKY ONE-GALLON BEER STEIN ANYWHERE?

CHECKMATE.

I WIN.
AMEND

HA HA HA HA HA HA HA HA HA HA HA HA...

THE PROBLEM WITH LAPTOPS IS THERE'S NO PLUG TO RIP OUT OF THE WALL.
ANOTHER GAME, CHUMP-BOY?

FoxTrot
BILL AMEND

MR. FOX, I'VE CHECKED AND NO ONE ELSE IN THIS DEPARTMENT USES № 2½ PENCILS. EFFICIENCY DEMANDS THAT ALL PENCILS IN THIS OFFICE BE THE SAME AND PURCHASED IN BULK. YOUR LITTLE PENCIL INDULGENCE IS UNNECESSARILY COSTING THIS COMPANY PENNIES EACH MONTH. **PENNIES!**

AMEND

THE NAME OF THE GAME IN BUSINESS, MR. FOX, IS EFFICIENCY. WASTED TIME IS WASTED MONEY.

TAKE, FOR EXAMPLE, THE WAY YOU ARE WALKING THROUGH THIS OFFICE: LEFT TURNS, RIGHT TURNS, UP THE STAIRS, DOWN THE STAIRS

IF YOU JUST STOPPED WEAVING ALL OVER THE PLACE, YOU'D GET WHER-EVER YOU'RE GOING IN HALF THE TIME!
AMEND

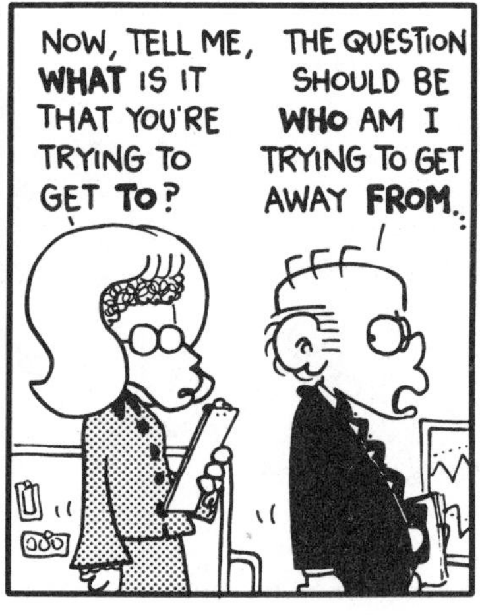
NOW, TELL ME, **WHAT** IS IT THAT YOU'RE TRYING TO GET **TO**?
THE QUESTION SHOULD BE **WHO** AM I TRYING TO GET AWAY **FROM**..

WHAT **IS** THIS?!
THE CENTERPIECE OF MY EFFICIENCY REVIEW.

I'VE NOTICED THAT WHEN YOU AND YOUR STAFF WORK ON THE COMPUTER, YOUR LEGS ARE UNOCCUPIED. IF WE COULD TRAIN YOUR PEOPLE TO TYPE WITH THEIR FEET ON A SECOND KEYBOARD, WE COULD LAY OFF HALF YOUR STAFF WITH NO LOSS IN PRODUC-TIVITY.
AMEND

OF COURSE, IF WE DOUBLE PEOPLES' WORKLOADS, WE'D PROBABLY HAVE TO GIVE THEM 10 PERCENT RAISES...

WHY DO I KEEP THINKING TODAY IS APRIL 1?
YOU KNOW, MY LAST CLIENT'S EYE HAD THAT EXACT SAME TWITCH.

WELL, MR. FOX, I'VE FINISHED MY REPORT ON WAYS TO MAKE YOUR DEPARTMENT MORE EFFICIENT.

BY MY BEST ESTIMATION, THE CHANGES I SUGGEST YOU IMPLEMENT WILL SAVE THIS OFFICE OVER $1,000 EACH YEAR.

WOW. THAT'S GREAT.
...LESS, OF COURSE, MY FEE FOR THIS PAST WEEK.

PLEASE TELL ME YOU FORGOT THE DECIMAL POINT.
LOOK, 11½ YEARS FROM NOW, YOUR COMPANY WILL THANK ME.
AMEND

FoxTrot
BILL AMEND

MOM! MOM! I GOT A 91 PERCENT ON MY MATH TEST!
WHY, PAIGE, THAT'S GREAT!
AMEND

IT'S THE BEST I'VE DONE ON A MATH TEST ALL YEAR! IT BRINGS MY AVERAGE UP TO A STRAIGHT "B"!
SEE WHAT HAPPENS WHEN YOU STUDY?

I'M IN SUCH A GOOD MOOD! NOTHING COULD DEPRESS ME RIGHT NOW!
MOM! MOM! I GOT A 108 PERCENT ON MY MATH TEST!

I ALWAYS SPEAK TOO SOON.
WHY, JASON, THAT'S GREAT!
IT'S A NEW SCHOOL RECORD!

O GREAT OUIJA BOARD...

PLEASE GRANT ME AN ANSWER TO THIS QUESTION...

"HOW HAS THE MONROE DOCTRINE SHAPED U.S. FOREIGN POLICY IN THE YEARS SINCE ITS ISSUANCE IN 1823?"

I FIGURE IT'S WORTH A SHOT.
PETER, WILL YOU JUST WRITE YOUR STUPID ESSAY?!
AMEND

fontSize:= 36;
FOR i:= 1 to 1000 DO
BEGIN
writeln('KICK ME');
writeln;
END;

PRINTZZZ... PRINTZZZ... PRINTZZZ... PRINTZZZ...

AMEND

YOU GOTTA LOVE THE PERSON WHO INVENTED FORM-FEED LABELS.
HIYA, TRACY. NICE JOB ON THAT REPORT LAST MONTH!
PAT PAT

BLINK
BLINK
BLINK

ZZZZZ...

WHUMP!
AMEND

I'VE REALLY GOT TO STOP NODDING OFF IN ART CLASS.

I JUST CAN'T FIGURE OUT THIS CREDIT CARD STATEMENT.
IN WHAT WAY?

IT'S BIZARRE. IT SHOWS A PURCHASE, THEN A CREDIT, THEN A PURCHASE, THEN A CREDIT, THEN A PURCHASE, THEN A CREDIT...

WHAT'S GOING ON?? IS IT A COMPUTER GLITCH?
DAD, THINK ABOUT IT.
AMEND

MOM, **PLEASE** DON'T MAKE ME TAKE THIS BACK!
PAIGE, THAT SWEATER COST MORE THAN MY COLLEGE TUITION!
HARPERS

MUNCH
MUNCH
MUNCH
MUNCH
AMEND

YOU KNOW... WHAT ARE CHOCOLATE CHIP COOKIES WITHOUT A GLASS OF MILK?

GLUG
GLUG
GLUG
GLUG

YOU KNOW... WHAT'S A GLASS OF MILK WITHOUT A FEW CHOCOLATE CHIP COOKIES?...

AAAAA!
AMEND

SCARY NOVEL?
ITTY-BITTY PRINTING.

HEY, PAIGE, I DIDN'T KNOW YOU AND JANE GOODALL WERE BUDDIES!
WHAT ARE YOU TALKING ABOUT?

THIS MAGAZINE HAS A PICTURE OF YOU TWO STANDING ARM-IN-ARM IN THE JUNGLE.
SHE HAS HER ARM AROUND A CHIMPANZEE!

OH. WHOOPS. MY MISTAKE.
THAT IS SO MEAN! GIVE ME THAT!
AMEND

HEY, PETER, I DIDN'T KNOW YOU AND JANE GOODALL WERE BUDDIES!
WHAT ARE YOU TALKING ABOUT?

OK, MY PRETTY VALENTINE, NOW CLOSE YOUR EYES...
YOU GOT ME FLOWERS?!

NO...
CHOCOLATES?!

NO...
JEWELRY?!?

ANDY, GEEZ! YOU'VE BEEN WANTING A NEW SPATULA FOR YEARS!
EVER WONDER, ROGER, WHY NONE OF OUR KIDS HAVE BIRTHDAYS IN NOVEMBER?
AMEND

BOING!
BOING!
BOING!
BOING!
BOING!

AMEND

NOPE. THE SPIDER'S STILL UP THERE.
MAYBE WE SHOULD GET A BIGGER SUPERBALL...

PAIGE, QUIT HOGGING THE POPCORN!
THERE'S PLENTY! CALM DOWN, YOU SPAZ!

YOU'VE EATEN HALF THE BOWL! LET ME HOLD IT FOR A CHANGE!
I'M THE ONE WHO MADE IT! LEGGO!

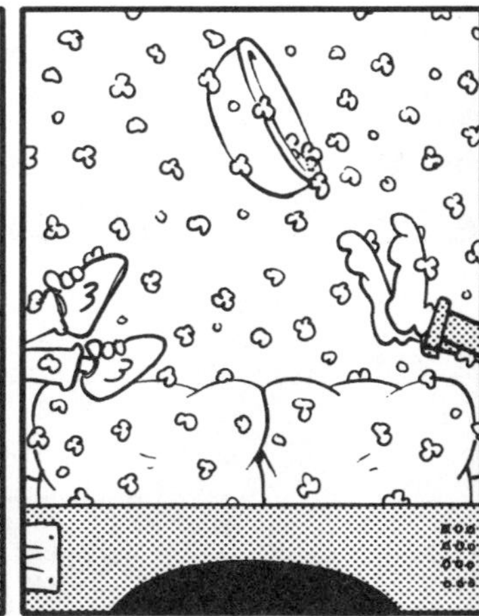

WHEN YOU FACTOR IN THE THREE HOURS OF CLEANING, I'M NOT SURE RENTING MOVIES IS ALL THAT GREAT A BARGAIN.
JASON, QUIT HOGGING THE ICE CREAM!
AMEND

Rodent Man

AMEND

MOM, THE CEILING'S DRIPPING!
THAT'S ODD. THE ONLY THING ABOVE YOU IS PAIGE'S BEDROOM.

I STILL CAN'T BELIEVE HUNKY JIMMY ANDREWS IS MOVING!
WA-AA!

FoxTrot

BILL AMEND

MOM, IS IT OK IF I SET OFF A FIRECRACKER INSIDE THE HOUSE?
ABSO-LUTELY NOT!

I PROBABLY SHOULD'VE ASKED BEFORE LIGHTING THE FUSE.

AN ONBOARD EXPLOSION SENDS DEEP SPACE NINE CAREENING OUT OF CONTROL!

WHEN SUDDENLY IT COLLIDES WITH A GIANT KLINGON BIRD OF PREY THAT HAD BEEN CLOAKED NEARBY!

THE TWO HULLS FUSE TOGETHER AND TUMBLE HELPLESSLY TOWARD A WHITE-HOT NEUTRON STAR!

WHOSE GRAVITATIONAL FIELD SLINGSHOTS THEM BACK IN TIME TO A LATE 20TH-CENTURY EARTH!

AS SISKO, ODO AND THE KLINGONS SURVEY THE DAMAGE, A CAR SLOWLY APPROACHES...

IT'S X-FILES AGENTS MULDER AND SCULLY! "THE TRUTH IS HERE!" SQUEALS MULDER.

WHAT I WOULDN'T GIVE TO BE A NETWORK EXECUTIVE.
WHAT SOME OF US WOULDN'T GIVE TO PREVENT IT.
I THINK MULDER SHOULD DRIVE THE CAR FROM "KNIGHT RIDER."
AMEND

JASON AND PETER ARE AT THE DENTIST... MOM'S RUNNING ERRANDS... DAD'S STILL AT WORK...

I CAN'T BELIEVE I'VE GOT THE ENTIRE HOUSE TO MYSELF! WEEEEEEEEEEE!

WHAT TIME DID THEY SAY THEY'D GET BACK?...
AMEND

QUINCY, SHOO!
Verlon

I MEAN IT! SHOO!

I'M TRYING TO READ! SHOO! SHOO! SHOO! SHOO! SHOO! SHOO! **SHOO!**
AMEND

HAS JASON TAUGHT YOU **NOTHING?!**

QUINCY, WILL YOU STOP EATING MY SHOELACE?!

OK, FINE. SWALLOW THE SHOELACE. SEE WHAT **I** CARE. YOU'LL PROBABLY CHOKE TO DEATH ON IT.

Hack! Hack! Gack!
Verlon

WHY CAN'T I EVER BE THIS RIGHT WHEN IT COMES TO THINGS LIKE SCHOOLWORK?
AMEND

LOOK AT THIS, QUINCY! YOU'VE GOT THE ENTIRE SHOELACE STUCK IN YOUR THROAT!

OK, IT'S OUT. YOU CAN BREATHE NOW. QUINCY? I SAID YOU CAN BREATHE NOW.

LET ME PUT IT THIS WAY, QUINCY—IT'S GROSS ENOUGH THAT I'M SITTING HERE HOLDING AN IGUANA...

...I'M NOT ABOUT TO BE HOLDING A DEAD ONE!
Gasp! Gasp! Cough! Gasp! Gasp!
AMEND

WELL, QUINCY, YOU'VE MADE THIS QUITE THE INTERESTING AFTERNOON.
AMEND

I JUST HOPE YOU'VE LEARNED YOUR LESSON.

THAT IS, IF YOU WANT TO LIVE, DON'T GO CHEWING ON SHOELACES.

I SHOULD WARN YOU, THE SAME GOES FOR CERTAIN NOSES.

JASON'S GONNA FREAK WHEN I TELL HIM I SAVED YOU FROM CHOKING.

I MEAN, I'M GONNA OWN THAT BOY! HE'LL DEDICATE HIS WHOLE LIFE TO THANKING ME!
AMEND

...OF COURSE, THAT PROBABLY MEANS HE'LL SPEND IT FOLLOWING ME AROUND...

ON SECOND THOUGHT, LET'S JUST KEEP THIS OUR LITTLE SECRET.

FoxTrot
BILL AMEND

WHAT'S THE WEATHER SUPPOSED TO BE LIKE TODAY?
LET'S SEE...

RAIN. LOTS OF IT. UP TO 10 INCHES EXPECTED.
Cartoonist Charms at White House Gala

GREAT.
ALL DAY LONG. RAIN, RAIN, RAIN, RAIN, RAIN...
AMEND

... IN GUATEMALA.
FIGURES THIS HAPPENS ON CLASS-PHOTO DAY.
Math

WHAT ARE YOU DOING?
MAILING FAN LETTERS TO MYSELF.

THIS WAY, WHEN I REALLY **DO** BECOME HUGELY IMPORTANT AND FAMOUS, I'LL BE USED TO THE ADULATION AND IT WON'T MESS WITH MY HEAD. I'D HATE FOR MY EGO TO GO BONKERS.

OF COURSE, THE MERE FACT THAT I'M DOING THIS MEANS IT'S PROBABLY TOO LATE.

I THINK "GOD-LIKE" IS TWO WORDS.
HI, I'D LIKE TO CANCEL ALL THOSE FLOWERS I ORDERED...
AMEND

SEE, THE HIGHLANDER IS AN IMMORTAL, WHICH MEANS HE CAN'T BE KILLED.
UH-HUH.

...UNLESS HE GETS HIS HEAD CHOPPED OFF, WHICH IS WHY THEY ALL CARRY SWORDS UNDER THEIR COATS.
AND YOU ACTUALLY **WATCH** THIS SHOW?!

WHAT? – IT'S COOL!

JASON, THAT IS THE MOST RIDICULOUS AND UNBELIEVABLE PREMISE FOR A TV SHOW THAT I'VE EVER HEARD OF! I CAN'T BELIEVE YOU BUY INTO THIS NONSENSE!

AMEND

SEE, BILLY AND ALLISON WERE **GOING** TO GET MARRIED, BUT THEN BILLY MARRIED BROOKE AND ALLISON MARRIED BROOKE'S DAD.
UH-HUH.

STEVE'S DAD SET UP THIS AMAZING HOME THEATER IN THEIR BASEMENT.

THEY'VE NOW GOT THIS BIG-SCREEN TV WITH FIVE-FOOT SPEAKERS ON EITHER SIDE, THX SURROUND SOUND AND THIS KILLER 200-WATT SUB-WOOFER. HE SHOWED THIS ONE SCENE FROM "JURASSIC PARK" AND I SWEAR, I THOUGHT WE WERE ACTUALLY GOING TO DIE, WHAT WITH ALL THE SHAKING.

THE DINOSAURS SEEMED THAT REAL?
NO, NO, I THOUGHT THE HOUSE WAS GOING TO COLLAPSE ON TOP OF US.

AND TO THINK I WASTED MY CHILDHOOD WATCHING MOVIES THAT EMPHASIZED PLOT.
STEVE SAYS WITH "DIE HARD III," YOU CAN SEE THEIR WINDOWS FLEX.
AMEND

THEY LOOK LIKE THEY FIT OK. HOW DO THEY FEEL?
NOT BAD. LET ME TEST THEM OUT.

SAY "HERE COMES YOUR SISTER IN NOTHING BUT HER UNDERWEAR."
AMEND

HERE COMES YOUR SISTER IN NOTHING BUT HER UNDERWEAR.
AIEEE!

YOU KNOW, I THINK I'VE SOLD YOU SHOES BEFORE.
DO YOU HAVE ANYTHING WITH A LITTLE MORE TRACTION?

AMEND

IF YOU THINK I'M GONNA FEEL GUILTY ABOUT ENJOYING THIS WEATHER...

FoxTrot

BILL AMEND

THE COMPUTER ATE MY COLUMN...

THE REFRIGERATOR LEAKED WATER ALL OVER THE KITCHEN...

THE CITY DECIDED OUR STREET WAS IN DESPERATE NEED OF JACKHAMMERING...
AMEND

COULD A DAY STINK ANY WORSE?
MIND IF I LIGHT THIS BABY UP BEFORE DINNER?

ROGER, WHAT IS THAT THING IN YOUR MOUTH?!
IT'S A CIGAR.

I KNOW **THAT**. WHAT ARE YOU DOING WITH IT?
FRED GAVE IT TO ME.

CHECK OUT THE FANCY LABEL: *AROMA DEL BAÑO.*

ROGER, DID YOU EVER STUDY SPANISH IN SCHOOL?
MY PRONUNCIATION IS THAT GOOD, EH?
AMEND

ROGER, I DON'T WANT THAT THING IN MY HOUSE.
ANDY, WHERE HAVE YOU BEEN? CIGARS ARE VERY HIP RIGHT NOW.

ROGER, I MEAN IT.
ALL THE YOUNG GUYS AT WORK ARE SMOKING THEM!
AMEND

YOU'RE NOT ONE OF THEM.
IT'S THE STYLE! IT'S THE TREND! IT'S THE RAGE!

YOU GOT THE "RAGE" PART RIGHT.
ANDY, C'MON– LET ME BACK IN...

OK, FINE! LOCK THE STUPID DOOR!
CLICK!

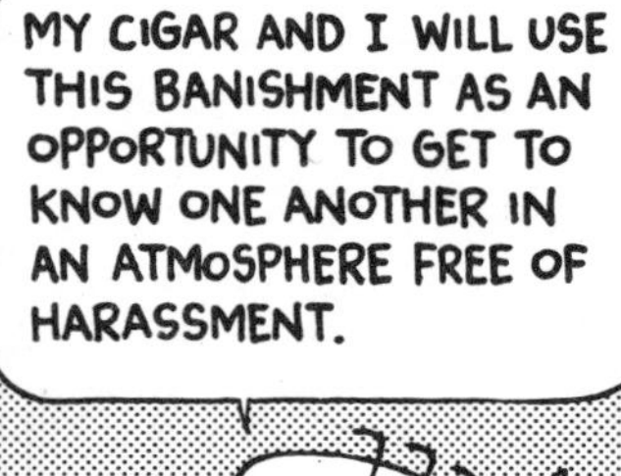
MY CIGAR AND I WILL USE THIS BANISHMENT AS AN OPPORTUNITY TO GET TO KNOW ONE ANOTHER IN AN ATMOSPHERE FREE OF HARASSMENT.

AMEND

PUFF PUFF PUFF PUFF

I'M SORRY– DID YOU SAY "HARASSMENT" OR "OXYGEN"?
HAR (COUGH) HAR (COUGH) HAR (COUGH)...

SEE, ANDY, A GOOD CIGAR HAS THE POWER TO TRANS-PORT YOU TO FARAWAY LANDS.

TAKE, FOR INSTANCE, THE CIGAR I'M ENJOYING RIGHT NOW...
AMEND

WITH ITS WOODY BOUQUET... ITS HEADY DRAW... ITS RUD-DY FLAVOR... TAKE A SNIFF AND TRY TO GUESS WHERE IT'S TAKING ME.

INDUSTRIAL NEW JERSEY?
NO, NO– THE CARIBBEAN, SILLY.

WHAT?? NO GOODNIGHT KISS??
ROGER, YOU STILL REEK OF THAT DISGUSTING CIGAR!

BUT I BRUSHED MY TEETH! I GARGLED WITH MOUTH-WASH! I WASHED MY HANDS! I CHANGED OUT OF MY CLOTHES!

WHAT MORE DO YOU WANT ME TO DO?!

I ASSUME YOU WERE KIDDING ABOUT THE LYSOL.
AMEND

FoxTrot
BILL AMEND

ICK. PEANUT BUTTER.
I CAN'T BELIEVE YOU AND I HAVE BEEN GOING OUT FOR OVER A YEAR NOW, DENISE.

403 DAYS.
SERIOUSLY, WHODATHUNKIT?

I MEAN, YOU'RE SMART AND FUNNY AND PRETTY AND WONDERFUL AND FRIENDLY AND THOUGHTFUL AND PERFECT AND WHAT AM I ?!
AMEND

PERCEPTIVE?
BY THE WAY, YOU'VE GOT SOME QUALITIES THAT I DIDN'T MENTION...

PETER, I THOUGHT MAYBE YOU COULD COME OVER AFTER DINNER TONIGHT.
SURE. JUST TO HANG OUT?

WELL, ACTUALLY, YOU SEE, MY PARENTS ARE GOING TO BE OUT AND I WAS HOPING WE COULD, UM...YOU KNOW...
AMEND

GEEZ, I FEEL LIKE SUCH A GEEK SAYING THIS...
I THINK I CAN GUESS WHAT YOU HAVE IN MIND.

I WANT TO STUDY FOR NEXT MONTH'S SATs.
THE ONE TEEN-AGER IN THE UNIVERSE WITH A WORK ETHIC AND SHE HAS TO BE MY GIRLFRIEND.

"MNEMONIC," PETER— WHAT'S IT MEAN?
SO, DENISE, WHAT TIME DID YOUR PARENTS SAY THEY'D BE BACK?

"ASPERSION," PETER— WHAT'S IT MEAN?
I MEAN, WAS IT SOON? LATER? LOTS LATER?...
AMEND

"ISOMORPHISM," PETER— WHAT'S IT MEAN?
...BECAUSE IF IT WAS LOTS LATER, WE'D HAVE TIME TO STUDY AND TO...

"SELF-CONTROL," PETER— WHAT'S IT MEAN?
EASY FOR YOU TO SAY— YOU DON'T HAVE TO LOOK AT ME.

LOOK, PETER, MY HORMONES ARE JUST AS ACTIVE AS YOURS ARE – IF NOT MORE SO – BUT THAT'S NOT THE ISSUE HERE.

THE POINT IS, WHEN I ASKED MY PARENTS IF YOU COULD COME OVER AND HELP ME STUDY, I HAD TO PROMISE THEM THAT THIS WOULDN'T TURN INTO ONE OF OUR USUAL KISSFESTS. I **TOLD** YOU THAT BEFORE YOU GOT HERE.
AMEND

SO NO SMOOCHING. I GAVE MY WORD. SORRY.

WHAT ABOUT PLAIN OL' GROPING?
PETER, I REALLY HOPE YOU'RE SMILING RIGHT NOW.

DENISE? WE'RE HOME.
OH, HI, DAD. PETER AND I ARE IN THE DEN.
SAT

WE'LL LEAVE YOU KIDS ALONE, THEN. HOW'D YOUR STUDYING GO?
PRETTY WELL. JUST A FEW THINGS LEFT TO DO.
AMEND

SMACK
MMPH!
SAT

I ONLY PROMISED THEM I WOULDN'T KISS YOU WHILE THEY WERE GONE.
AIR... GASP... AIR... GASP...

YOU KNOW, DENISE, I REALLY WISH I HAD YOUR WILLPOWER.

I TOTALLY WAS MR. HORMONES TONIGHT. IT WAS LIKE I COULDN'T EVEN **THINK** ABOUT STUDYING! I FEEL LIKE SUCH A LOSER.
AMEND

I WISH I HAD YOUR WILL-POWER... I WISH I HAD YOUR SELF-CONTROL... I WISH I HAD YOUR WORK ETHIC AND INTEGRITY AND ALL THOSE THINGS I **DON'T** HAVE.
BUT YOU **DO** HAVE THEM, IN A WAY.

...YOU HAVE **ME**.
WHAT CONCERNS ME, THOUGH, IS THAT YOU'VE GOT **ME**.

FoxTrot
BILL AMEND

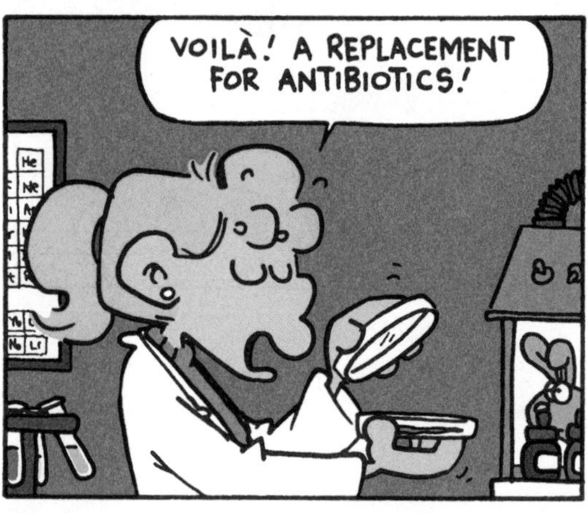

WHERE'S PAIGE? I HAVEN'T SEEN HER ALL AFTER-NOON.
SHE AND NICOLE WENT TO THE LIBRARY. I THINK THEY'RE RESEARCHING COLLEGES.

COLLEGES?
YOU KNOW, TRYING TO FIGURE OUT WHICH ONES THEY WANT TO APPLY TO.
Sports Nut

(SNIFF) OH, PETER... A MOTHER LIVES FOR MOMENTS LIKE THIS. MY LITTLE GIRL HAS FINALLY DECIDED TO TAKE ACADEMICS SERIOUSLY.
AMEND

ICK. NOTRE DAME'S COLORS TOTALLY CLASH WITH MY SKIN TONE.
STANFORD'S RED WOULD GO GREAT WITH THOSE CUTE SHOES YOU BOUGHT.
GUIDE TO COLLEGES

I COMMAND THIS RAIN TO STOP!

I COMMAND THIS RAIN TO STOP!

I COMMAND THIS RAIN TO—...
AMEND

SOME PROOFS OF OMNIPOTENCE ARE INEVITABLE.
WHERE HAVE YOU BEEN FOR THE LAST SIX HOURS?!

LET'S HOPE THEY NEVER PUT MY SISTER'S IMAGE ON A COIN.
WHY'S THAT?
GOPHER MAN
Raptor Boy

THERE'D BE NO WAY TO TELL THE HEAD FROM THE TAIL!
WAAA HA HA HAR HEE HEE!
GOPHER MAN

OH, MAN, PAIGE WOULD KILL ME IF SHE EVER HEARD THAT.
New Gopher Man T-Shirts!
GOPHER MAN

WHAT DO YOU MEAN SHE'S NOT HOME?!
AMEND

UM, PAIGE, I WAS SICK YESTERDAY AND I WAS WONDERING...

...UM, WAS WONDERING WHAT CHAPTERS WE WERE SUPPOSED TO...

...UM... SUPPOSED... TO... UM...

I KNEW IT WAS A MISTAKE TO EAT SOUR PATCH KIDS AT SCHOOL.
SO, UM, ARE YOU BUSY FRIDAY NIGHT?
AMEND

SLURRRP...

AMEND

P-P-PAIGE, AB-B-BOUT THIS COFFEE YOU M-M-MADE...
I ALWAYS FORGET- IS IT A TEASPOON OF GROUND COFFEE FOR EACH CUP OF WATER, OR VICE VERSA?

WHAT ARE YOU DOING?
MODIFYING THIS VIDEO GAME.

DOOMATHON HAS THIS UTILITY PROGRAM THAT LETS YOU CREATE YOUR OWN MONSTERS AND WEAPONS. CHECK OUT THIS HEAT-SEEKING BAZOOKA I DESIGNED.

AND CHECK OUT THE CREATURES I'LL BE USING IT ON...

I SEE YOU'VE WISELY MADE ABOUT 25 BACK-UP COPIES.
PAIGE'S YEARBOOK PHOTO WAS BLACK AND WHITE, SO THE GREEN MAY BE A LITTLE OFF...
AMEND

FoxTrot
BILL AMEND

SO YOU GOT ROPED INTO DOG-SITTING. BIG DEAL. I THOUGHT YOU LIKED DOGS.
I DO, BUT THIS DOG IS PSYCHOTIC!
Verlon
GLAM

HE'S THIS MINUSCULE LITTLE THING THAT I OUTWEIGH BY LIKE 200-TO-1 AND COULD CRUSH WITH MY BIG TOE, YET ALL HE DOES IS ATTACK ME OVER AND OVER AND OVER!

IT'S LIKE HE'S BRAIN-DAMAGED OR SOMETHING!
Verlon
GLAM
AMEND

ACTUALLY, I CAN RELATE.
YOU CAN?
YO, PAIGE, PREPARE TO EAT RUBBER.
M-1000

FAUNTLEROY?

IT'S PETER FOX. REMEMBER ME? I'M HERE TO FEED YOU DINNER.
YIP! YIP! YIP! YIP! YIP!

YES, IT'S GOOD TO SEE YOU TOO, FELLA.
YIP!

IT'S GOING TO BE A LONG WEEK.
Grrrr Grrr Grrrr Grrr Grrrr
Gourmet DOG CHOW
AMEND

OK, FAUNTLEROY, HERE'S YOUR GRUB.
YIP! YIP! YIP! YIP! YIP! YIP! YIP!

WHY AREN'T YOU EATING? AM I DOING THIS WRONG?
YIP! YIP! YIP! YIP! YIP! YIP! YIP! YIP!

LET'S SEE... "FEEDING INSTRUCTIONS"...

YOU KNOW, I DIDN'T EVEN KNOW THEY MADE BELLS OUT OF CRYSTAL.
Ding-a-ling-a-ling
SLURP MUNCH SLURP
AMEND

FAUNTLEROY, LET GO OF MY LEG!
Grrrrrr

I MEAN IT! LET GO!
Grrrrr

LISTEN, YOU PSYCHOTIC LITTLE RAT-DOG, IF YOU DON'T STOP CHEWING ON MY LEG THIS INSTANT, I'M GOING TO PUNT YOU LIKE A BONY LITTLE FOOTBALL INTO GOD KNOWS WHAT TIME ZONE!

OK, SO TECHNICALLY YOU DID OBEY ME...
Grrrrr
AMEND

YES, FAUNTLEROY, IT'S ANOTHER DOG.
YIP! YIP! YIP! YIP! YIP! YIP! YIP!

YES, FAUNTLEROY, HE'S WITHIN 50 MILES OF YOUR HOUSE.
YIP! YIP! YIP! YIP! YIP! YIP! YIP! YIP! YIP! YIP!
AMEND

YES, FAUNTLEROY, YOU HAVE EVERY RIGHT TO TELL HIM TO SCRAM.
YIP! YIP! YIP! YIP! YIP! YIP! YIP! YIP! YIP!

I'M GUESSING, FAUNTLEROY, THAT YOUR ANCESTORS MUST HAVE PROCREATED VERY, VERY QUICKLY.
YIP! YIP! YIP! YIP!

MRS. TAFT WANTS TO KNOW IF YOU AND FAUNTLEROY HAD FUN THIS WEEK.
DID WE HAVE FUN?!

EVERY TIME I WENT OVER THERE, THAT STUPID LITTLE PIRANHA-DOG SUNK HIS FANGS INTO MY LEGS! WHY DO YOU THINK I'VE BEEN LIMPING?! HE SHREDDED MY PANTS... HE CHEWED UP MY SOCKS...

AND DID I TELL YOU WHAT UNSPEAKABLE THING HE DID TO MY SNEAKERS ON THURSDAY?!

FOR WHAT IT'S WORTH, MRS. TAFT, I'VE HAD FUN THIS WEEK.
I MEAN, THESE USED TO BE WHITE!
AMEND

FoxTrot

BILL AMEND

Welcome to the Jason Fox World Wide Web Home Page!!!

• To view a photo of Jason, click here.

This is me, Jason Fox. I like science, math and Plasma Man comic books.

• To view a photo of my iguana, click here.

This is Quincy, my iguana. He likes to escape from his cage and eat things.

• To view a photo of my friend Marcus, click here.

This is my best friend, Marcus. He's pretty cool. We're a lot alike.

• To view a photo of my Saturn V model, click here.

This is the Saturn V rocket I built. Marcus wants to put his hamster on board.

• To view a photo of my sister Paige, click here.

IN ACCORDANCE WITH THE INDECENCY STATUTES OF THE 1996 FEDERAL TELECOMMUNICATIONS ACT, THE IMAGE OF MY SISTER'S OBSCENELY UGLY FACE IS NO LONGER AVAILABLE FOR PUBLIC VIEWING AT THIS SITE.

• For the next best thing, click here.

METHINKS THE WEB HAS GOTTEN JUST A WEE TOO ACCESSIBLE.
WHY'S IT NOW LINKING ME TO THE COLUMBUS ZOO CHIMP FACILITY?
AMEND

NOW, MOM, DON'T FREAK OUT, BUT SOME GUYS ON THE BASE-BALL TEAM LOST A BET WITH SOME GUYS ON THE SOCCER TEAM, AND...
CULTURE STUFF

WELL...
AMEND

YOU SHAVED YOUR HEAD? HOW CUTE.

HEY, PAIGE, WE WERE WRONG – SHE DIDN'T GO BALLISTIC.
NOW TAKE OFF THAT SILLY BALD WIG AND GET READY FOR DINNER.
CULTURE STUFF

YOU MEAN THIS **WASN'T** AN APRIL FOOL'S JOKE?!

YOU REALLY **DID** SHAVE YOUR HEAD?!
AMEND

AAAA! MY BEAUTIFUL SON! YOU LOOK LIKE A SKINHEAD!

PEOPLE WILL THINK YOU'RE A NAZI!
MICHAEL JORDAN HAS A SHAVED HEAD AND NO ONE CALLS **HIM** A NAZI...

PETER, HOW COULD YOU **DO** THIS?!

HOW COULD YOU AND YOUR FRIENDS MAKE SUCH A STUPID BET?!

WHAT ON EARTH WERE YOU THINKING?!
AMEND

IT'S A PUZZLEMENT.
YOUR FATHER'S GOING TO LOVE THIS.

SO THE SOCCER TEAM DID THIS TO YOU AND YOUR BASEBALL TEAMMATES.
UM, YEAH.

BECAUSE YOU LOST SOME STUPID BET ABOUT WHO COULD EAT THE MOST TRIPLE BURGERS IN AN HOUR.
BASIC-ALLY.

SON, I'M GOING TO SAY SOMETHING THAT MAY SOUND A LITTLE INSENSITIVE, BUT...

I'M NOT THE BALDEST GUY IN THIS HOUSE ANYMORE! YEE-HA!
YOU KNOW, I THINK I'LL GO LET MOM CHEW ME OUT SOME MORE.
AMEND

JASON, I SAID NO.
PLEEEEASE??

NO!
PLEASE? PLEASE? PLEASE? PLEASE? PLEASE? PLEASE? PLEASE? PLEASE? PLEASE? PLEASE? PLEASE? PLEASE?

OK, FINE. BUT JUST THIS ONE TIME!

AHEAD, WARP FACTOR SEVEN. ENGAGE.
GOOSE BUMPS.
AMEND

CHECK OUT ALL MY PEACH FUZZ!

AND THIS IS ONLY SINCE MONDAY!

I'LL BET IN ANOTHER WEEK OR TWO, I'LL SIMPLY LOOK LIKE A KID WITH A CREW CUT!

ISN'T IT GREAT THE WAY HAIR JUST GROWS RIGHT BACK?
LOOK, I'M SORRY I MADE FUN OF YOU, OK?!
AMEND

FoxTrot
BILL AMEND

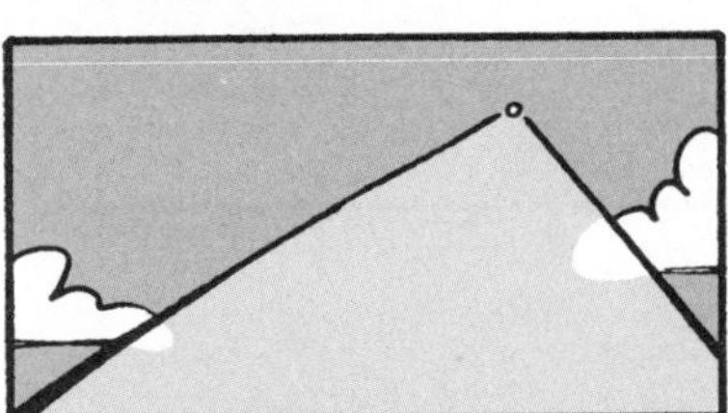

BAM!

YOU KNOW, THAT WOULD HAVE BEEN PRETTY IMPRESSIVE HAD I ACTUALLY BEEN AIMING FOR THAT CAN.
SON, WHY DON'T WE LAY OFF THE KNUCKLEBALLS FOR A WHILE.
DON'T MOST PITCHERS AT LEAST HIT THE BACKSTOP?
AMEND

MOM, DO YOU REMEMBER THAT "BRADY BUNCH" EPISODE WHERE PETER BUILDS A VOLCANO OUT ON THEIR BACK PATIO?
SORT OF.

THEY SHOW IT ALL THE TIME– YOU KNOW, WHERE IT BLOWS UP AND MUDDY GOOP GOES FLYING ALL OVER HIS SISTER AND IT'S REALLY FUNNY?

WOULD IT BE OK WITH YOU IF I DID SOMETHING LIKE THAT?
YOU WANT TO BUILD A VOLCANO TO HURL GOOP AT YOUR SISTER?
AMEND

ACTUALLY, I PLANNED TO SKIP THE "VOLCANO" PART...
JASON, WHAT'S IN THAT BUCKET?
IS THIS BLOUSE WHITE OR WHAT?

ROGER, THERE'S A MR. STARK HERE TO SEE YOU.

OH, MAN! NOT **ANOTHER** SALES PITCH!

WHY CAN'T THESE SALES-MEN LEAVE ME ALONE?! WHY CAN'T THEY SEE THAT I'M BUSY?! WHY CAN'T THEY COME AROUND ONCE A YEAR INSTEAD OF EVERY OTHER DAY?! **WHY?!**
AMEND

...AND WHY CAN'T I EVER SAY NO?
ROGER, ROGER! YOU'RE GIVING ME WRITER'S CRAMP!

YOUR "DARK FORCES" CD-ROM WAS IN MY AEROSMITH CASE.
THAT MIGHT EXPLAIN WHY THESE ALIENS LOOK SO FUNNY.
AMEND

MMM – ANDY, THIS SOUP IS REALLY GOOD!

I MEAN, SERIOUSLY, THIS IS HEAD AND SHOULDERS ABOVE ANYTHING YOU'VE EVER COOKED BEFORE!

WHAT IS IT?
IT'S A COMPOUND TO SEAL THE CRACKS IN THE DRIVEWAY.

PLEASE TELL ME IT'S POISONOUS.
NOW, ABOUT MY COOKING...
AMEND

PETER, YOU DIDN'T COME TO A COMPLETE STOP AT THAT STOP SIGN.
I STOPPED ENOUGH.

YOU COASTED RIGHT THROUGH IT! THE SPEEDOMETER NEVER WENT UNDER 5 MPH! MOM'S GOING TO HAVE A FIT WHEN SHE HEARS ABOUT THIS!

...IF SHE HEARS ABOUT THIS.
AMEND

I MUST SAY, YOUR STOPPING SKILLS ARE IMPROVING.
ONE JUNIOR DINO-DOG AND A BLUE-CHOCOLATE SHAKE, PLEASE.
(BZZT) PULL UP TO THE SECOND WINDOW.

HOLE 1
AMEND

HOLE 1

CRACK!
HOLE 1

APPARENTLY, I NEED TO LOOSEN UP BEFORE I LOOSEN UP.
LEMME GRAB YOU A SHORTER CLUB.

FoxTrot

BILL AMEND

BUT WAS HE **REALLY** KING? WAS HE **REALLY** THE MOST POWERFUL AND FEARED OF THE DINOSAURS? NEXT SLIDE, PLEASE.

IT IS MY CONTENTION THAT THE PLANT-EATING PACHYCEPHALOSAURUS WAS, IN FACT, THE **TRUE** KING OF THE LATE CRETACEOUS. HOW IS THIS POSSIBLE, YOU ASK?

A COMPARISON OF ITS HEAD WITH THOSE OF THE TELEPATHIC TALOSIANS FEATURED IN STAR TREK'S "THE CAGE" EPISODE SUGGESTS STRONGLY THAT THESE CREATURES POSSESSED EXTRA-ORDINARY PSYCHIC ABILITIES.

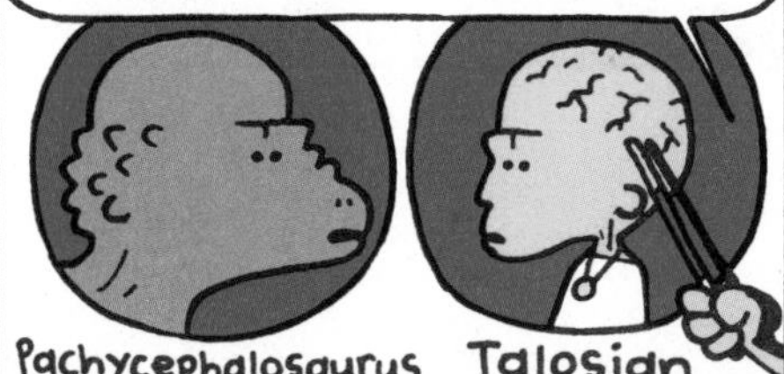

TYRANNOSAURS, VELOCIRAPTORS AND OTHER PREDATORS MORE THAN LIKELY WERE TURNED INTO "THOUGHT SLAVES" BY THESE ALL-POWERFUL PACHYS... GIANT, MEAT-EATING PUPPETS READY TO OBEY THEIR MASTERS' EVERY WHIM.

NOW, THEN, WHY DID DINOSAURS EVENTUALLY GO EXTINCT? MY THEORY: TIME-TRAVELING BIG-GAME HUNTERS. MY EVIDENCE? NEXT SLIDE.

PETER, YOU SAID YOU'D STRAIGHTEN UP YOUR ROOM TODAY!
I WILL, BUT I WANT TO WORK ON MY JUMP SHOT FIRST.

PAIGE, YOU SAID YOU'D HELP ME PUT IN NEW SHELF PAPER!
I KNOW, BUT NICOLE WANTS ME TO MEET HER FOR ICE CREAM.

JASON, YOU SAID YOU'D PICK UP THAT MESS YOU MADE IN THE BASEMENT.
MOM, GEEZ- THESE ARE IDEAL LAUNCH CONDITIONS!

THE PROBLEM WITH SPRING CLEANING IS THAT IT'S IN THE SPRING.
I PROMISE I'LL START ON THE ATTIC JUST AS SOON AS I'M DONE WITH GOLF...
AMEND

YOUR SON'S BEEN A REGULAR MISTER SUPER-CLEANER TODAY.
JASON?

YUP. HE PICKED ALL THOSE DEAD FLIES OUT OF THE WINDOWSILLS... HE CHECKED ALL THE MOUSETRAPS UP IN THE ATTIC... HE EVEN WENT THROUGH THE FRIDGE LOOKING FOR SPOILED FOOD.

I JUST HOPE HE THROWS IT ALL AWAY.
WHAT ELSE WOULD HE DO WITH IT?

I MADE YOU A BAG LUNCH, PAIGE.
WHAT'S THAT SMELL?
Fourteen
AMEND

FIT!

FIT!
FIT!
AMEND
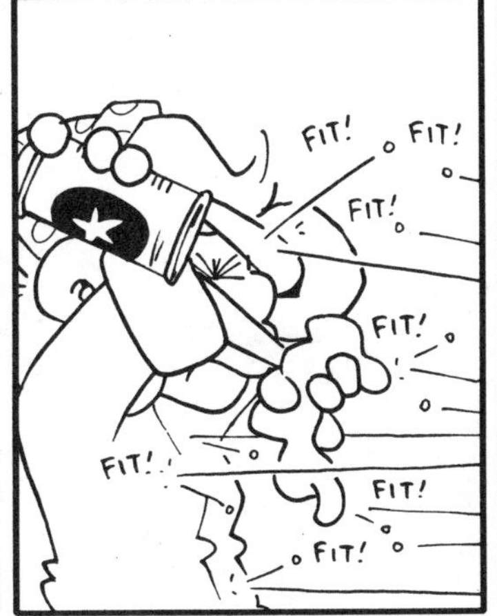
FIT! FIT!
FIT!
FIT!
FIT!
FIT!
FIT!

PAIGE, PUT A BAG IN THE VACUUM CLEANER!
DIRTSUCKER 2000

AND YOU, PETER, THROUGHOUT THIS WHOLE WEEK, HAVE DONE ABSOLUTELY NOTHING. WHAT DO YOU HAVE TO SAY FOR YOURSELF?

AMEND

FoxTrot
BILL AMEND

SPORTS NUT

BUT JAI ALAI'S AN INDOOR SPORT!
THE KID HAS A POINT.
ROGER!
AMEND

HEY, PETER, LOOK WHAT I FOUND IN THE BASEMENT!
OH, YEAH– THAT'S MY OLD MAGIC SET.
Toridos
Magic

I GOT IT FOR MY BIRTHDAY ABOUT FIVE YEARS AGO. I NEVER REALLY USED IT MUCH.
AMEND

IF YOU DON'T WANT IT, CAN I HAVE IT?
SURE. WHY NOT?
Magic
Toridos

WELL, JASON, YOU'VE CERTAINLY ANSWERED MY QUESTION.
C'MON–IT'LL JUST LOOK LIKE I'M CHOPPING OFF YOUR FINGERS...

I FIGURED OUT WHAT I'M GOING TO DO FOR A LIVING.
OH?

I'M GOING TO BE THE WORLD'S GREATEST MAGICIAN! I'LL DO TV SPECIALS! LIVE SHOWS! I'LL FILL STADIUMS! WHAT A LIFE!

DID YOU KNOW THAT DAVID COPPERFIELD MAKES AN EIGHT-FIGURE INCOME?

OF COURSE, HE ALSO HAS SUPERMODELS THROWING THEMSELVES AT HIM.
I SUPPOSE THERE ARE DOWNSIDES TO EVERYTHING.
AMEND

WHY THE LONG FACE?
PETER GAVE ME HIS OLD MAGIC SET, BUT ALL THE TRICKS IN IT ARE REALLY LAME.
Mr. Magic

LOOK AT THIS JUNK – CUPS AND BALLS... SPONGE RABBITS... A HANDKERCHIEF THAT CHANGES COLOR... THEY CALL THIS MAGIC?!
Mr. Magic

WHERE'S THE FIRE?! WHERE ARE THE TIGERS?! WHERE'S THE BED OF SPEARS I CAN DANGLE MYSELF OVER WHILE I TRY TO GET OUT OF LEG IRONS?!
Mr. Magic
AMEND

DEAR, I TAKE BACK ALL THOSE JOKES ABOUT YOUR HAIR GOING GRAY.
WHAT I REALLY NEED IS A GOOD STRAIT-JACKET.
Mr. Magic

Brickstone's SECRETS OF MAGIC

FLIP FLIP FLIP
Brickstone's SECRETS OF MAGIC

Brickstone's SECRETS OF MAGIC

SOMEHOW I EXPECTED MORE BARGAINING WITH THE DEVIL AND FEWER WIRES AND MIRRORS.
ONLY YOU WOULD SEEM DISAPPOINTED BY THIS.
AMEND

WANT TO SEE MY DEATH-DEFYING STRAITJACKET ESCAPE? I'VE BEEN PRACTICING IT ALL AFTERNOON.
SURE.
SPORTS NUT

OOF... UGGH... ALMOST THERE... OOF... HERE WE GO...
AMEND

TA DA!
WHERE'S THE DEFYING-DEATH PART?

THAT'LL COME WHEN PAIGE SEES WHAT THIS HAS DONE TO HER SWEATER.
HAVE YOU CONSIDERED WORKING UP A GOOD VANISHING ACT?

AND NOW, THE MOMENT YOU'VE ALL BEEN WAITING FOR! I REACH INTO MY HAT AND PRODUCE NOT ONE, BUT—...
The Great Jasoni

UM...
AMEND

SHOOT—WHERE'D THEY ALL GO?
WHERE'D WHAT ALL GO?
he Great Jasoni

WELL, MARCUS, I FIGURED OUT WHY MAGICIANS DON'T TYPICALLY WORK WITH SNAKES...

FoxTrot

BILL AMEND

Tweeee!
I SWEAR, EVERYONE'S A CRITIC.

OK, EVERYONE, HOLD ON TO YOUR SEATS!...
A
M
M
M
3

...BECAUSE YOU ARE ABOUT TO EXPERIENCE A NEW TASTE SENSATION KNOWN AS EGGS À LA PAIGE!

NOT FRIED... NOT SCRAMBLED... BUT SOMEWHERE DELIGHTFULLY IN BETWEEN.

WITH A DELICATE CHEESE TOPPING AND BIG HUNKS OF BEEF THROUGHOUT.

ACTUALLY, ALL OUR BEEF WAS FROZEN, SO I USED BOUILLON CUBES INSTEAD.

I'VE ALSO WHIPPED UP A BATCH OF ORANGE JUICE À LA PAIGE.

THEY NEVER HOLD ON TO THEIR SEATS.
A
B
3
AMEND